KEY

A NEW

GRAMMAR

OF THE WRITTEN LANGUAGE

By J. A HAYWOOD

Senior Lecturer in Arabic, University of Durham

and H. M. NAHMAD, B.Litt.(Oxon.)

LUND HUMPHRIES

Published by
Lund Humphries
Wey Court East,
Union Road,
Farnham,
Surrey GU9 7PT

ISBN 978-0-85331-068-6

First edition 1964
Reprinted with corrections 1976
Reprinted 1979
Reprinted 1987
Reprinted 1990
Reprinted 1997
Reprinted 1999
Reprinted 2002
Reprinted 2005
Reprinted 2009

A New Arabic Grammar of the Written Language
replaces Thatcher's *Arabic Grammar*
which is no longer available
This *Key* replaces the *Key to Thatcher's Arabic Grammar*

Printed and bound in Great Britain by
CPI Antony Rowe, Chippenham, Wiltshire

PREFACE

The response to "A New Arabic Grammar" has already been very gratifying to the authors. But some disappointment has been expressed at the lack of a Key giving model translations of the exercises.

In point of fact, the grammar was intended primarily as a teaching grammar, not as a "teach yourself" work. It is already being used in universities and similar institutions in Great Britain and the Commonwealth, and (through the Harvard University Press Edition) in North America. There has also been some demand from other European, Asian and African countries.

It has become clear that the grammar is also being used as a means of learning Arabic by many who have no teacher, and it is chiefly for their benefit that this key has been prepared. It is being sold as an optional extra for those who require it.

The danger of a key is that students may refer to it too readily. It should, ideally, be used merely as a check to students' work after they have done it unaided.

One other general point may be mentioned here: the more advanced the work becomes, the greater are the possibilities of alternative translations. In these model translations some alternatives are given, but they are not exhaustive. They are, moreover, kept within the compass of the vocabulary and text of the grammar. For further details, the Introduction should be consulted.

The authors trust that this key may serve a useful purpose, and invite suggestions for subsequent editions.

J.A.H.
H.M.N.

INTRODUCTION

The following points should assist students in using this Key.

A TRANSLATION FROM ARABIC INTO ENGLISH

1. A sound rule of accurate translation is to *keep as near as possible to the original, without abusing the language into which one is translating.* Needless inaccuracy – as, for example, writing "I found *a* book" where the Arabic original says "*the* book" – is inexcusable. But, English translations must be in idiomatic English.

In this Key, where the English idiom diverges considerably from the Arabic original, a literal translation of the Arabic is frequently given, after the idiomatic translation, in brackets, preceded by the abbreviation *lit.*

The authors, in giving literal translations, have borne in mind the fact that some users of the grammar may know English only as a *second language*, and may therefore be not quite so familiar with some English idioms as native English speakers.

On the other hand, literal translations are inserted much less in later exercises than in the early ones.

2. There are often two or more alternative translations, each as acceptable as the other. Alternative translations are here given in brackets, preceded by *or* in italics.

In this connection, it must be stressed that no effort has been made to indicate every possible alternative.

Often, with isolated sentences, alternative translations are due to the lack of a context. For example, the third person masculine singular perfect of *taraka*, to leave, may mean "he left", "he has left", or even "he had left", according to the context. After a conditional particle, it could mean if he "leaves", "were to leave", "left", "has left" or "had left". To include all these alternatives would increase the bulk of this Key without greatly helping the student.

Another instance is in the use of the definite article. As Arabic frequently uses the definite article for generalisation, the same sentence may mean "I like coffee (in general)" or "I like *the* coffee" (to which reference has presumably already been made).

In the above and similar connections, the rule of the authors in this Key has been to include some common alternatives in the early stages, but to omit them later. The student must use his common sense, or just make an individual choice, in determining his own translation.

3. One matter deserving special stress is that of Arabic conjunctions. It is the Arab custom to link sentences by *wa*, *fa* and *thumma*, whereas in English it is considered bad style to begin sentences with "and". In these translations, therefore, the word "and" is frequently omitted at the beginning of sentences.

4. Abbreviations used in this Key are those of the grammar itself. The chief are:—

sing.	singular	*pl.*	plural
masc.	masculine	*fem.*	feminine

also *lit.*, literally, as mentioned above.

B TRANSLATION FROM ENGLISH INTO ARABIC

5. The general remarks on accuracy in translation in paragraph 1 above apply here also.

6. Alternative translations are inserted in brackets without any other indication. These include two important categories:—

(a) Common synonyms, such as the different words for "garden".

(b) Nouns which may be either masculine or feminine (see pages 28 and 368 in the Grammar). Adjectives agreeing with such nouns may, of course, be in either gender.

7. Occasionally optional interpolations are inserted in brackets, with no other indication. The authors hope that these will be so obvious, that the reader will not confuse them with the alternatives mentioned in paragraph 6 above.

8. The general aim has been to keep this Key as short, simple, and unpretentious as possible. Only in rare instances has it been felt necessary to include explanatory notes on translation problems. There is undoubtedly need for a book on advanced translation to and from Arabic. But this would be far beyond the scope of this strictly utilitarian Key to "A New Arabic Grammar".

Exercise 1

1. I am small (*or* young) and you are big (*or* old). 2. You are a tall man. 3. The street is wide and long. 4. The Nile is a river, it is a big river. 5. The door is old. 6. The house is beautiful (*or* attractive, nice). 7. A short river. 8. The narrow sea. 9. A nice (*or* good, handsome) boy. 10. Tea and coffee. 11. The tea and the coffee. 12. I am a man and you are a boy. 13. The chair is small. 14. The cup is old, it is broken. 15. The book is beautiful, it is new. 16. The door is broken. 17. A man, a boy, and a girl. 18. I and she. 19. You and he. 20. The narrow street.

Exercise 2

١- اَلْبَيْتُ كَبِيرٌ . ٢- بَيْتٌ كَبِيرٌ . ٣- رَجُلٌ طَوِيلٌ وَوَلَدٌ قَصِيرٌ . ٤- حَسَنٌ وَلَدٌ صَغِيرٌ . ٥-اَلنَّهْرُ ضَيِّقٌ . ٦- شَارِعٌ وَاسِعٌ . ٧- هُوَ وَلَدٌ جَدِيدٌ . ٨-بَابٌ مَكْسُورٌ عَتِيقٌ . ٩- اَلنِّيلُ نَهْرٌ طَوِيلٌ وَاسِعٌ .١٠- اَلْكِتَابُ جَدِيدٌ . ١١- كِتَابٌ جَدِيدٌ . ١٢- اَلْبَحْرُ جَمِيلٌ .١٣ كُرْسِيٌّ قَدِيمٌ . ١٤- شَايٌ حَسَنٌ . ١٥- قَهْوَةٌ قَدِيمَةٌ .١٦-اَلْفِنْجَانُ صَغِيرٌ. ١٧-رَجُلٌ وَوَلَدٌ . ١٨- أَنْتَ رَجُلٌ طَوِيلٌ وَأَنَا قَصِيرٌ . ١٩-كِتَابٌ صَغِيرٌ جَدِيدٌ . ٢٠-اَلشَّارِعُ اَلطَّوِيلُ

1

Exercise 3

1. The beautiful new clock (*or* watch) is broken. 2. Is it a large clock (*or* watch)? 3. No, it is (a) small (one). 4. The mother is present. 5. The bride is a beautiful girl. 6. Bad (*or* ugly) writing. 7. A new Caliph. 8. Is the girl beautiful? Yes! 9. A clean foot. 10. The earth (*or* land) is wide (*or* extensive). 11. Damascus is a hot place. 12. The house is distant and the sun is hot (*lit.* strong). 13. The grandfather is dead. 14. The (female) servant is present. 15. A tall tree. 16. Ḥasan is a fine man, he is a doctor. 17. The garden is far. 18. A great (*or* big, old) king. 19. A beautiful queen. 20. The queen is beautiful.

Exercise 4

١- أَنْتِ جَمِيلَةٌ . ٢- اَلشَّجَرَةُ ٱلطَّوِيلَةُ مَيِّتَةٌ . ٣- اَلأُمُّ
حَاضِرَةٌ . ٤- هَلِ ٱلْعَرُوسُ حَاضِرَةٌ ؟ لَا ! ٥- اَلْخَلِيفَـةُ
ٱلْمَيِّتُ . ٦- اَلْخَلِيفَةُ مَيِّتٌ . ٧- رِجْلٌ طَوِيلَةٌ . ٨- أَرْضٌ
وَاسِعَةٌ . ٩- دِمَشْقُ بَعِيدَةٌ . ١٠- اَلسَّاعَةُ ٱلْقَدِيمَـةُ
مَكْسُورَةٌ . ١١- هِيَ بِنْتٌ قَبِيحَةٌ . ١٢- أَنْتِ ٱلْمَلِكَةُ . ١٣-
اَلْمَلِكُ رَجُلٌ جَمِيلٌ . ١٤- أَأَنْتِ (هَلْ أَنْتِ) ٱلْجَدَّةُ ؟ لَا، أَنَا
ٱلأُمُّ . ١٥- كِتَابَةٌ قَبِيحَةٌ . ١٦- رِجْلٌ كَبِيرَةٌ . ١٧- هَـلِ
ٱلْبُسْتَانُ نَظِيفٌ ؟ نَعَم ، هُوَ نَظِيفٌ . ١٨- هُوَ طَبِيبٌ .

2

١٩- طَرِيقٌ وَاسِعٌ (وَاسِعَةٌ) طَوِيلٌ (طَوِيلَةٌ) . ٢٠-ٱلْبَيْتُ
ٱلْجَدِيدُ صَغِيرٌ .

Exercise 5

1. There are a plate and a knife on the table (*or* a plate and knife are on the table).   2. The boy's clean spoon.   3. The milk is nice.   4. From the old market.   5. To the market of Mecca.   6. Ḥasan's son is a well-behaved (*lit.* upright) boy. 7. Muḥammad's daughter is in honest Ḥasan's garden.   8. The king of Egypt is a just king.   9. He is the son of the angry king.   10. You are angry with Ḥasan, and he is a nice boy.   11. The bread is old and the meat is tough (*lit.* strong).   12. The butter is from the milk of Muḥammad's cow.   13. The Caliph's mother's fork is on the small table. 14. Mecca is a fine place.   15. You are in handsome (*or* beautiful) Ḥasan's garden.   16. The table is in a house of Muḥammad's.   17. The bread is on the new plate; it is with the butter.   18. Is the milk fresh (*or* new)? No, it is stale (*or* old).   19. You are in the king's garden.   20. The boy's tea is in the large cup.

Exercise 6

١- ٱلْمَلِكُ زَعْلَانُ مِنَ ٱلْوَزِيرِ ٱلْجَدِيدِ . ٢- فِي بَيْتِ حَسَنٍ
مَائِدَةٌ جَمِيلَةٌ جَدِيدَةٌ . ٣- عَلَى ٱلْمَائِدَةِ سِكِّينٌ
وَشَوْكَةٌ وَمِلْعَقَةٌ . ٤- ٱلْحَلِيبُ (ٱللَّبَنُ) مَعَ ٱلْخُبْزِ وَٱلزُّبْدِ
(وَٱلزُّبْدَةِ) . ٥- سُوقُ دِمَشْقَ ٱلْجَدِيدُ (ٱلْجَدِيدَةُ) فِي شَارِعٍ

3

طَوِيلٍ ضَيِّقٍ . ٦- اَللَّحْمُ عَلَى ٱلصَّحْنِ . ٧- هُوَ رَجُلٌ حَسَنٌ

عَادِلٌ مِنْ مَكَّةَ . ٨- اِبْنُ ٱلْمَلِكِ ٱلصَّغِيرِ فِي بَيْتِ لِلْوَزِيرِ .

٩- جَدَّةُ ٱلْخَلِيفَةِ مَيِّتَةٌ . ١٠- أُمُّ حَسَنٍ ٱلْجَمِيلَةُ طَبِيبَةٌ .

١١- أَفِي (هَلْ فِي) ٱلْبَيْتِ نَارٌ؟ ١٢- هَلْ فِي بَيْتِ ٱلرَّجُلِ

كُرْسِيٌّ شَدِيدٌ؟ ١٣- أَفِي (هَلْ فِي) ٱلْفِنْجَانِ ٱلْكَبِيرِ قَهْوَةٌ

جَدِيدَةٌ؟ ١٤- اَلسِّكِّينَةُ (اَلسِّكِّينُ) وَٱلشَّوْكَةُ لِلْوَزِيرِ .

١٥- أَنَا رَجُلٌ عَادِلٌ وَأَنْتَ خَادِمٌ أَمِينٌ . ١٦- أَنَا مِنْ مِصْرَ .

١٧- دِمَشْقُ جَمِيلَةٌ . ١٨- مَلِكُ مِصْرَ رَجُلٌ عَادِلٌ . ١٩- نَعَمْ

هُوَ رَجُلٌ قَصِيرٌ . ٢٠- سَاعَةُ ٱلطَّبِيبِ ٱلْقَدِيمَةُ ٱلْمَكْسُورَةُ

مَعَ ٱلْكِتَابِ عَلَى ٱلْمَائِدَةِ .

Exercise 7

1. There are many languages in the world.   2. They (two)
are tailors.   3. There were two bakers in the house (*lit.* two
bakers were in the house).   4. The teachers are present.
5. There are many difficult words in Ḥasan's book.   6. The
believers are absent today.   7. They were in the street
yesterday; today they are in the house (*or* at home).   8. The
new year (has) arrived.   9. There are two windows in the

house. 10. He asked the two cooks for food. 11. The
Caliph wrote to the believers in Damascus. 12. He asked
for an animal, and a man arrived. 13. The sick minister
attended the meeting. 14. The book is easy to the doctor.
15. Is there a wild animal in the teacher's garden? 16. She
asked the servants for bread, butter, tea, and milk. 17.
There are many Muslims in Egypt. 18. Are they (*fem. pl.*)
Muslims? 19. The two Ḥasans' garden has two gates (*or*
doors). 20. The two books were on the table yesterday.
Today they are in the doctor's house.

Exercise 8

١- لُغَتَانِ صَعْبَتَانِ . ٢- كَتَبَ كِتَابَيْنِ سَهْلَيْنِ لِلْوَلَـدِ .

٣- وَصَلَ ٱلْفَنْبُ مِنَ ٱلْخَبَّازِ أَمْسِ . ٤- ٱكْلُ ٱلطَّبَّاخَيْنِ ٱلْآخِرَيْنِ

ٱلْيَوْمَ جَمِيلٌ . ٥- ٱلْمُعَلِّمُونَ ٱلْمُسْلِمُونَ غَائِبُونَ ٱلْيَـوْمَ .

٦- كَانَ بَيْنَا لِمُؤْمِنَيْنِ . ٧- لِبَيْتِ حَسَنٍ شُبَّاكَـانِ

(نَافِذَتَانِ) وَبَابَانِ وَبُسْتَانٌ كَبِيرٌ . ٨- هُمَا رَجُلَانِ مَرِيضَانِ

ضَعِيفَانِ . ٩- فِي ٱلْعَالَمِ حَيَوَانَاتٌ وَحْشَةٌ كَثِيرَةٌ . ١٠- حَضَرُوا

ٱجْتِمَاعَاتٍ* كَثِيرَةٍ . ١١- طَلَبُوا خَيَّاطِينَ طَيِّبِينَ . ١٢- كَلِمَتَانِ

---

* (i) The word اِجْتِمَاع begins with *hamzatu l-waṣl* (see Chapter One,
7b). When beginning a sentence, however, it is pronounced with an
initial *kasra* as if written إِجْتِمَاع . In the sentence given above the *ū* of
حَضَرُوا اجتماعات is immediately followed, in pronunciation, by the *j* of اجتماعات.
(ii) اجتماع takes the sound feminine plural as is usual with nouns not
referring to male human beings, and which have no broken plural;
(see last paragraph on page 42 of the Grammar). This word is actually
the verbal noun (infinitive) of the verb "to assemble, gather together".

5

١٣- صَغِيرَتَانِ . ١٤- فِي ٱلْكِتَابِ كَلِمَاتٌ صَعْبَةٌ كَثِيرَةٌ .

وَصَلَا مِنْ مِصْرَ أَمْسِ . ١٥- أَنْتُمَا مُعَلِّمَانِ . ١٦- نَحْنُ

مُسْلِمُونَ صَالِحُونَ . ١٧- هُنَّ مُعَلِّمَاتٌ بِدِمَشْقَ (فِي

دِمَشْقَ) . ١٨- سِنُونَ (سَنَوَاتٌ) كَثِيرَةٌ . ١٩- يَوْمَانِ . ٢٠- أَنَا

وَأَنْتَ طَبِيبَانِ طَيِّبَانِ . هُوَ طَبِيبُ ٱلْحَيَوَانَاتِ .

Exercise 9

1. They found many dogs in the market yesterday. 2. The Arab girl wrote (*or* has written) beautiful English letters. 3. You killed two men with the sword two months ago (*lit.* before two months). 4. Many long ships left (*or* have left) Suez. 5. (The) Arabic lessons are useful (*or* profitable) to the students. 6. The dog is a watchful animal. 7. The students were in Cairo a few months ago. 8. Then they went to Damascus. 9. The minister has a swift servant. 10. The rainy season (*lit.* times of the rains) is long in India. 11. The students left the lessons an hour ago. 12. They are difficult studies (sciences). 13. They (two) found (some) beautiful mountains far from the city. 14. Are (the) swords profitable (*or* useful)? 15. No, (the) books are profitable. 16. Muḥammad has a sharp (*or* cutting) sword, and Ḥasan has a righteous heart. 17. They are the old (*or* great, big) men, and we are the small (*or* young) boys. 18. It is a difficult river for (the) big ships. 19. Two girls arrived and demanded (*or* asked for) bread and milk from the (maid-)servant. 20. We are difficult men.

6

١- ذَهَبَ الطُّلَّابُ إِلَى بُيُوتِ الْمُعَلِّمِينَ. ٢- خَرَجُوا مِنَ الدُّرُوسِ قَبْلَ سَاعَتَيْنِ. ٣- بَعْدَ وَقْتٍ طَوِيلٍ وَصَلَ الْمُعَلِّمُونَ الْجُدُدُ. ٤- هِيَ أَنْهُرٌ سَرِيعَةٌ. ٥- وَصَلَ أَوْلَادٌ إِنْكِلِيزٌ قَلِيلُونَ الْيَوْمَ فِي السَّفِينَةِ الْكَبِيرَةِ. ٦- هُمْ مِنْ مُدُنٍ كَثِيرَةٍ. ٧- قَتَلَ الْمَلِكُ الْوَزِيرَ بِالسَّيْفِ ثُمَّ خَرَجَ إِلَى الْجَبَلِ. ٨- فِي بَيْتِ مُحَمَّدٍ كَلْبٌ حَارِسٌ. ٩- وَجَدُوا الْوَلَدَ الْعَرَبِيَّ قَبْلَ سَاعَةٍ. ١٠- كُتُبُ حَسَنٍ سَهْلَةٌ. ١١- حَضَرَ الطُّلَّابُ الدُّرُوسَ أَمْسِ. ١٢- أَشْهُرٌ طَوِيلَةٌ. ١٣- لِلْبَقَرِ قَلْبٌ كَبِيرٌ. ١٤- ذَهَبَ وَقْتُ الْأَمْطَارِ. ١٥- حُرُوفُ الْأَوْلَادِ الْعَرَبِيَّةُ قَبِيحَةٌ. ١٦- كَانَ سَيْفٌ قَاطِعٌ فِي يَدِ الرَّجُلِ الطَّوِيلِ. ١٧- طَلَبُوا عِلْمًا (الْعِلْمَ) فِي مِصْرَ. ١٨- الْقَاهِرَةُ وَدِمَشْقُ مَدِينَتَانِ كَبِيرَتَانِ. ١٩- هُمَا مَدِينَتَانِ عَرَبِيَّتَانِ. ٢٠- وَصَلَتِ السُّفُنُ الْكَبِيرَةُ الْجَدِيدَةُ فِي الْإِسْكَنْدَرِيَّةِ مِنْ لَنْدَنَ قَبْلَ يَوْمَيْنِ.

Exercise 11

1. There was a sceptre in the king's hand an hour ago.
2. The English ambassador mentioned the good news about the ships. 3. Ḥasan's rich friends are present in the house with the Arab prince's relations. 4. The girl took beautiful jewels from the minister. 5. Muḥammad is the Prophet of the Arabs. 6. They are in the sultan's council today. 7. They attended the council in the prince's house. 8. She found many beautiful books in (some) old trunks (or boxes). 9. Cairo, Alexandria and Tanta are big towns in Egypt. 10. The ambassador had (*lit.* took) a cup of tea in the minister's house. 11. The man found the letters on the new desk. 12. (The) news arrived from the minister, or from the king. 13. The pupils arrived at (the) school. 14. The pupils' handkerchiefs are clean today. 15. The teachers' (*or* professors') experiments are useful (*or* profitable). 16. The ambassador's son and the prince's sister are friends. 17. Has the sultan's mother heard (*lit.* known) today's news? 18. No, she left the city two days ago. 19. You are the rich (ones). 20. He mentioned the books of the prophets.

Exercise 12

١- وَصَلَ ٱلْخَبَرُ عَنِ ٱلتَّجَارِبِ مَجْلِسَ ٱلْوُزَرَاءِ أَمْسِ (وَوَصَلَ مَجْلِسَ ٱلْوُزَرَاءِ أَمْسِ ٱلْخَبَرُ عَنِ ٱلتَّجَارِبِ) . ٢- هُمْ أُمَرَاءُ صَالِحُونَ . ٣- اَلسَّفِيرُ ٱلْجَدِيدُ صَدِيقُ ٱلْأَغْنِيَاءِ . ٤-هُوَ قَرِيبٌ مِنَ ٱلْمَدِينَةِ . ٥- كَانَتْ جَوَاهِرُ فِي ٱلصَّنَادِيقِ ٱلْقَدِيمَةِ . ٦- ذَكَرَ ٱبْنُ ٱلْمَلِكِ ٱلْأَخْبَارَ ٱلْحَسَنَةَ فِي

ٱلْمَجْلِسِ ٱلْيَوْمَ. ٧- ٱلْفَنَاجِينُ ٱلنَّظِيفَةُ فِي ٱلصَّنَادِيقِ ٱلْكَبِيرَةِ. ٨- أَخَذَ ٱلْأُسْتَاذُ أَبْنَاءَ ٱلْمَلِكِ إِلَى ٱلْمَدْرَسَةِ. ٩- حَضَرَتْ أُمَّهَاتُ ٱلتَّلَامِيذِ مَعَ ٱلْمُعَلِّمِينَ. ١٠- بَلَغَتْهُمُ ٱلْأَخْبَارُ عَنْ مَكَاتِيبِ ٱلسُّلْطَانِ. ١١- هُوَ مَعَ صَدِيقِ حَسَنٍ فِي ٱلْمَكْتَبِ. ١٢- هُمْ فِي بُسْتَانِ بَيْتِ مُحَمَّدٍ. ١٣- ذَهَبُوا إِلَى ٱلْقَاهِرَةِ أَوْ (إِلَى) دِمَشْقَ قَبْلَ شَهْرَيْنِ. ١٤- هِيَ ٱبْنَةُ ٱلْمَلِكِ وَأُخْتُ ٱلْأَمِيرِ. ١٥- قَتَلَ ٱلْأَقْرِبَاءُ ٱلسَّفِيرَ وَخَرَجُوا مِنَ ٱلْبَيْتِ. ١٦- وَجَدَتْ فَنَاجِينَ قَدِيمَةً فِي ٱلْبَيْتِ. ١٧- هِيَ مَنَادِيلُ قَدِيمَةٌ. ١٨- طَلَبَ شَايًا فِي فِنْجَانٍ نَظِيفٍ. ١٩- ٱلْأَغْنِيَاءُ (ٱلرِّجَالُ ٱلْأَغْنِيَاءُ) حَاضِرُونَ. ٢٠- هَلْ أَنْتُمْ أَنْبِيَاءُ؟

Exercise 13

1. The teacher's small (*or* young) son fell on the ground.
2. The merchant carried the new books and went to the school. 3. The women saw the boys' (*or* sons') teachers in the city street. 4. He is a very wealthy man, and he is un-intelligent (*lit.* little of intellect). 5. They are (female) cooks in the king's kitchen. 6. The mother put a morsel of meat and a piece of bread on the table. 7. They saw Muḥammad's

rich father. 8. The prince found the minister's two sons in a
small room in the palace (*or* castle). 9. The princess's eyes
are very pretty (*or* beautiful). 10. The tailors of Damascus
are good. 11. A wooden chest and an iron chest were in the
<u>Sh</u>aikh's house. 12. She is with Ḥasan's brother. 13. They
(two) saw the face of the householder (*or* master of the
house) then went (away). 14. They are two tribes of Iraq.
15. The boys' teachers are nice people. 16. The minister
killed the king's two sons yesterday. 17. She has a big mouth.
18. They saw the two windows of the house from far off.
19. The women are the cooks in the Arabs' houses. 20. The
teacher asked for two boys' watches for a useful experiment.

Exercise 14

١- فِي جُنَيْنَةِ ٱلشَّيْخِ ٱلْوَسِعَةِ قِطَعٌ كَثِيرَةٌ مِنْ خَشَبٍ
(ٱلْخَشَبِ). ٢- وَقَعَتْ لُقْمَتَا لَحْمٍ (لُقْمَتَانِ مِنْ لَحْمٍ
مِنَ ٱللَّحْمِ or) مِنَ ٱلْمَائِدَةِ عَلَى ٱلْأَرْضِ. ٣- مُعَلِّمُو
ٱلْمَدْرَسَةِ ٱلْجَدِيدَةِ ٱلْكَبِيرَةِ حَسَنُونَ. ٤- هُوَ رَجُلٌ
ذُو مَالٍ. ٥- أَنْتَ قَلِيلُ ٱلْعَقْلِ. ٦- شُيُوخُ ٱلْقَاهِرَةِ
أَصْحَابُ عِلْمٍ. ٧- طَلَبَتِ ٱلْاِمْرَأَةُ خُبْزًا مِنَ ٱلتَّاجِرِ.
٨- فِي حُجْرَةِ ٱلرَّجُلِ صُنْدُوقُ حَدِيدٍ. ٩- وَضَعَ كِتَابَيِ
ٱلسُّلْطَانِ ٱلْقَدِيمَيْنِ عَلَى ٱلْمَائِدَةِ ٱلْكَبِيرَةِ. ١٠- وَجَدَ
رَجُلًا ذَا عِلْمٍ مِنْ دِمَشْقَ فِي ٱلسُّوقِ. ١١- بَلَغَتْ

أَمْسِ أَخْبَارُ ٱبْنَيِ ٱلْوَزِيرِ مِنَ ٱلْمَدِينَةِ. ١٢- كَتَبَ
ٱلرَّجُلَانِ لِلتَّاجِرِ وَطَلَبَا خَشَبًا لِلْمَطْبَخِ. ١٣- لِسَانُ
ٱلْبَقَرِ طَوِيلٌ (طَوِيلَةٌ). ١٤- نَظَرَ ٱلْوَلَدُ وَجْهَ أَبِي مُحَمَّدٍ
فِي شُبَّاكِ ٱلْبَيْتِ. ١٥- وَصَلَ صَاحِبُ ٱلْبَيْتِ وَقَتَلَ
كَلْبَيِ ٱلشَّيْخِ. ١٦- خُبْزُ خَبَّازِي ٱلْقَاهِرَةِ جَمِيلٌ. ١٧-
هُنَّ نِسَاءٌ جَمِيلَاتٌ (جَمِيلَةٌ). ١٨- وَصَلَ مُعَلِّمُو
حَسَنٍ ٱلْيَوْمَ. ١٩- كَتَبَ ٱلرَّجُلُ مَكْتُوبَيْنِ طَوِيلَيْنِ
لِلْوَزِيرِ. ٢٠- كَانَتْ تَجْرِبَتَانِ نَافِعَتَانِ فِي ٱلْمَدْرَسَةِ
ٱلْيَوْمَ.

Exercise 15

1. Have you (*feminine*) opened the doors there? 2. Yes, I opened them (some) hours ago, then I closed them again two minutes ago. 3. The women entered and found their sons. 4. We (have) found many new books in Abū Bakr's shop. 5. What is your name? My name is Ḥasan, and my father's name is Muḥammad. 6. The schoolgirls (*lit.* girls of the school) rode their bicycles from their homes (*lit.* houses) to the market. 7. The king arrived from the palace by car (*lit.* by or in his car). 8. The shaikhs (*or* old men) rode their donkeys and horses. 9. The boy wrote a long letter with his pen and ink on his brother's paper. 10. The king's soldiers found gold and silver in the minister's house and killed his slave. 11. They found me between my enemy and my

11

friend. 12. I have many pounds at home (*lit.* in the house).
13. I have two man-servants and a maid-servant. 14. You
struck his head yesterday. 15. Why have you left your house?
Its walls are dirty. 16. You are sad. What are you thinking
about ? (*lit.* what is in your hearts). 17. The small boys hit
the roof of the house with stones. 18. The world is difficult
today. 19. Zaid was here yesterday with his sons. 20. The
shopkeepers closed their shops at noon.

Exercise 16

١- فَتَحَ صَدِيقُكَ ٱلشَّبَابِيكَ وَقَفَلَ ٱلْبَابَ قَبْلَ
سَاعَةٍ. ٢- وَجَدَنِي مُعَلِّمِيَّ فِي ٱلشَّارِعِ مَعَ حِصَانِ
أَبِي. ٣- ضَرَبَنِي عَلَى رَأْسِي. ٤- سَيَّارَتِي (عَرَبَتِي)
سَرِيعَةٌ جِدًّا. ٥- ٱلْحُجْرَةُ صَغِيرَةٌ وَسَقْفُهَا قَدِيمٌ
وَوَسِخٌ. ٦- لِمَاذَا رَكِبْتُمْ عَجَلَاتِكُمْ (دَرَّاجَاتِكُمْ)
لِلْمَدْرَسَةِ ٱلْيَوْمَ؟ ٧- بَلَغَتْنِي ٱلْأَخْبَارُ عَنْكَ أَمْسِ.
٨- ٱلْعَدُّقُ هُنَاكَ عِنْدَ بَابِ ٱلْمَدِينَةِ. ٩- مَعِي جُنَيْهَانِ
ٱلْيَوْمَ وَمَعَهُ جُنَيْهٌ. ١٠- ٱلْأُمُّ حَاضِرَةٌ هُنَا وَأُوْلَادُهَا
ٱلْكَثِيرُونَ فِي ٱلْمَدْرَسَةِ. ١١- خَرَجَتِ ٱلْمُعَلِّمَاتُ مِنَ
ٱلْمَدْرَسَةِ وَقَفَلْنَ أَبْوَابَهَا. ١٢- لِمَاذَا رَكِبْتُمْ
حَمِيرَكُمْ مِنْ بُيُوتِكُمْ إِلَى ٱلْمَدِينَةِ؟ ١٣- مَاذَا كَتَبْتَ

12

بِقَلَمِكَ عَلَى الْوَرَقِ ؟ ١٤- قَالَ لِلنِّسَاءِ : وَصَلْتُنَّ قَبْلَ
دَقِيقَةٍ . ١٥- رَأْسُهُ كَبِيرٌ وَرِجْلَاهُ صَغِيرَتَانِ. ١٦-حَائِطُ
الْحُجْرَةِ وَسَقْفُهَا وَبِطَانُهَا . ١٧- الْبَنَاتُ فِي دُكَّانِ أَبِيهِنَّ
فِي السُّوقِ . ١٨- دَخَلْتُ بَيْتَهَا (فِي بَيْتِهَا) وَضَرَبَتْنِي . ١٩-
تَرَكْتُمَا فِي الشَّارِعِ بَعِيدَةً عَنْ بَيْتِهَا . ٢٠- فِي مِصْرَ مُدُنٌ
جَمِيلَةٌ كَثِيرَةٌ ، لَهَا شَوَارِعُ وَاسِعَةٌ .

Exercise 17

1. This useful book has only just arrived (*lit.* has not arrived until the hour). 2. This is a difficult book. 3. The teacher entered and said to one of the pupils: "These books of yours are very dirty". 4. I found these two girls in that house. 5. Did you attend that council yesterday? 6. These persons killed his young sons. 7. That tree is shady. 8. Those men are learned. 9. That famous man left the city and has not returned up to now. 10. The people knew the reason for this calamity, so they closed their doors. 11. This calamity of yours is due (*lit.* from reason of) your neglect. 12. Who is this woman? She is (one) of the absentees. 13. How many boys did the teachers leave in (the) school after the lessons? 14. Which woman is present in that shop? 15. Who has ridden my horse, and has not closed the door? 16. He studied agriculture in Cairo University. 17. This mosque is famous in the East and the West. 18. The inhabitants of this village demanded new houses and a large school. 19. Why are you present and they absent?

NOTE: Sentences 17–19 are wrongly numbered 18–20 in the Grammar.

١- هَلْ عَرَفْتَ ذَلِكَ ٱلرَّجُلَ ٱلْمَشْهُورَ؟ لَا، عَرَفْتُ أَخَاهُ

ٱلْكَبِيرَ. ٢- هٰذَا رَجُلٌ طَيِّبٌ وَتِلْكَ ٱمْرَأَةٌ قَبِيحَةٌ.

٣- هٰذِهِ ٱلشَّجَرَةُ ذَاتُ ظِلٍّ حَسَنٍ .٤- هٰؤُلَاءِ ٱلْعَرَبُ

أَشْخَاصٌ طَيِّبُونَ .٥- أُولَئِكَ ٱلرِّجَالُ مَا وَصَلُوا حَتَّى

ٱلسَّاعَةِ. ٦- وَصَلَتْ هٰذِهِ ٱلْاِمْرَأَةُ مِنَ ٱلْقَاهِرَةِ أَمْسِ.

٧- أَيُّ رَجُلٍ وَجَدْتَ فِي تِلْكَ ٱلْحُجْرَةِ؟ ٨- أَيَّةُ ٱمْرَأَةٍ

قَتَلَتْ أَبَا ٱلْوَزِيرِ؟ ٩- كَمْ شَخْصًا حَضَرَ ٱجْتِمَاعَ ٱلْمَجْلِسِ

أَمْسِ؟ ١٠- مَا (مَاذَا) طَلَبْتَ مِنْ طُلَّابِكَ فِي ٱلْجَامِعَةِ؟

١١- هٰذَا جَامِعُ ٱلْمَدِينَةِ ٱلْكَبِيرُ. ١٢- وَجَدْتُ هٰذِهِ

ٱلْكُتُبَ فِي دُكَّانِ مُحَمَّدٍ فِي ٱلسُّوقِ ٱلصَّغِيرِ. ١٣- هٰذِهِ

مُصِيبَةٌ كَبِيرَةٌ لِسُكَّانِ قَرْيَتِي .١٤- لِكُلِّ هٰذَا سَبَبَانِ،

سَيْفُ ٱلْعَدُوِّ وَغَفْلَةُ ٱلْأَمِيرِ. ١٥- حَسَنٌ ٱبْنُ مَنْ؟

(ٱبْنُ مَنْ حَسَنٌ؟). هُوَ ٱبْنُ ٱلْوَزِيرِ. ١٦- هٰذَانِ ٱلرَّجُلَانِ

صَدِيقَانِ وَذَانِكَ عَدُوَّانِ .١٧- ٱبْنَةُ ٱلشَّيْخِ تِلْكَ

جَمِيلَةُ ٱلْوَجْهِ . ١٨- رَكِبَ ٱلرَّجُلَانِ حِصَانَيْهِمَا فَخَرَجَا مِنَ ٱلْمَدِينَةِ . ١٩- هَٰذِهِ سَيَّارَةٌ إِنْكِلِيزِيَّةٌ جَدِيدَةٌ . ٢٠ - دَرَسْنَا ٱلزِّرَاعَةَ مِنْ هَٰذَيْنِ ٱلْكِتَابَيْنِ ٱلْجَدِيدَيْنِ .

Exercise 19

1. This beautiful girl arrived from Baghdad a few months ago. She is the most beautiful girl in that famous city.
2. The colour of her face is white. 3. The black slave was in the blue room. 4. The teacher said to his pupils: "Why have you written your lessons in (the) green ink?" 5. In the villages of the east I found deaf women and dumb men!
6. This beggar is blind and lame, and he is yellow of colour.
7. The king is more just, so the inhabitants are happier than their fathers. 8. It is the greatest calamity in the history of the world up to now (*lit.* today). 9. A (*lit.* the) patient father is better than an angry one. 10. The tired pupil left the lesson; (and) he is the most ignorant boy in the school.
11. The new teacher left the very lazy boy in school after lessons. 12. The prince's army entered the city from the north, so the king's soldiers went out from the south, and left the inhabitants to the enemies' swords. 13. The man saw the most beautiful girl in the longest street in the town, and stopped at once. 14. This man's black hair is more attractive (*lit.* beautiful) than your white hair. 15. This road is more difficult than that, it is the most difficult of the roads of Syria. 16. The White and Blue Nile are the sources of the great Nile, and it is the river of Egypt. 17. The women went to the far frontier(s) of the country (*or* the frontier(s) of the far country). 18. Most of the people attended the meeting yesterday. 19. The woman's black eyes are very large. 20. The camel is better than the horse for the inhabitants of the desert.

١- هُوَ شَرٌّ مِنْ أَبِيهِ وَجَدُّهُ شَرُّ رَجُلٍ فِي ٱلْقَرْيَةِ. ٢- عَيْنَا

أُمِّي زَرْقَاوَانِ وَعَيْنَاىَ خَضْرَاوَانِ. ٣- ٱلْبَحْرُ ٱلْأَحْـمَرُ

حَدُّ بِلَادِ ٱلْعَرَبِ (جَزِيرَةُ ٱلْعَرَبِ) فِي ٱلْغَرْبِ وَٱلْجَنُوبِ.

٤- وَجَدْتُ كِتَابًا أَحْسَنَ مِنْ ذَلِكَ فِي مَكْتَبَةِ ٱلْمَدِينَةِ.

٥- بَيْتِي أَوْسَعُ مِنْ بَيْتِكَ، هُوَ أَوْسَعُ (ٱلْبَيْتُ ٱلْأَوْسَعُ)

بَيْتٍ بِبَغْدَادَ (فِي بَغْدَادَ). ٦- وَقَفَ ٱلْمُؤَلِّفُ فِي ٱلِٱجْتِمَاعِ

وَقَالُوا: نَحْنُ أَسْعَدُ مِنْكُمْ. ٧- هَذَا ٱلْوَلَدُ جَهُولٌ (جَاهِلٌ

جِدًّا)، وَذَلِكَ كَسُولٌ (كَسْلَانُ جِدًّا) مُعَلِّمُهُمَا غَضْبَانُ

مِنْهُمَا ٨- طَلَبَ ٱلسَّائِلُ ٱلْأَعْمَى ٱلْأَحْدَبُ ٱلْكَلَأَ مِنَ

ٱلنِّسَاءِ. ٩- وَصَلَ أَمْسِ مِنَ ٱلْجَنُوبِ ٱلْأَبْعَدِ وَدَخَلَ

دِمَشْقَ. ١٠- رَكِبْتُ حِصَانِي ٱلْأَحْمَرَ وَٱلشَّيْخُ رَكِبَ

جَمَلًا أَبْيَضَ. ١١- وَقَفَ جَيْشُ مِصْرَ فِي شَمَالِ صَحَارَى

بِلَادِ ٱلْعَرَبِ. ١٢- ٱلرِّجَالُ أَقْوَى مِنَ ٱلنِّسَاءِ. ١٣- لِحَسَنٍ

ٱلْمَوْلُ شِعْرِ ٱلطُّلَّابِ. ١٤- ضَرَبَ أَبِي أَكْبَرَ وَلَدٍ وَتَرَكَ

الأَصْغَرَيْنِ. ١٥- دَرَسَ الطُّلَّابُ أَسْهَلَ الكُتُبِ عَنْ
أَصْلِ الحَيَوَانَاتِ فِي الجَامِعَةِ. ١٦- مَنْ فَعَلَ أَجَدَّ شُبَّاكٍ
فِي البَيْتِ؟ ١٧- فَتَحَ البَابَ وَدَخَلَ الحُجْرَةَ فَذَهَبَ
بِأَجَدِّ صَحْنٍ وَأَحْسَنِ مِلْعَقَةٍ مِنَ المَائِدَةِ. ١٨- هٰذَا
الحَلِيبُ (اللَّبَنُ) أَقْدَمُ مِنْ ذٰلِكَ. ١٩- رَجَـعَ الجُنْدِيَّانِ
الأَطْوَلَانِ وَرَكِبَا الكُبْرَى الحِصْنِ (الحِصَانَـيْنِ
الأَكْبَرَيْنِ). ٢٠- هٰذَانِ المَجْهُولَانِ طَلَبَا خَيْرَ كُتُبٍ فِي
دُكَّانِ الكُتُبِ.

Exercise 21

1. Have you written (*or* did you write) the letter? 2. No,
I have not written (*or* did not write) the letter. 3. Have you
(*plural*) understood what we said (*lit.* our speech)? 4. Yes,
we have understood what you said. 5. The sun has risen
(*or* rose). 6. The moon has waned. 7. The tourist and
his servant travelled towards Damascus, and entered the
city. 8. We went out of the city gate (*lit.* the gate of the
city). 9. The men went up the mountain and came down.
10. Have you drunk the water? 11. No, we have not
drunk the water, we have drunk the wine. 12. Have you
and your brother broken the tumbler? (*lit.* glass of the water).
13. No, we have not broken the tumber. 14. I sent these
peasants (*or* cultivators) to the governor's house. 15. You
returned (*or* have returned) to your father's house. 16. The
house was about half an hour's distance. 17. I travelled
towards this house, and found its owners rich (*lit.* from the
rich). 18. The owner of the house opened the courtyard

17

gate to (*or* for) him. 19. On this day (*or* today) I went out hunting (*lit.* to the hunt). 20. They received the guest at their house this evening (*or* tonight). 21. The youth was glad, and asked the man for (the) food.

Exercise 22

١- أَكَتَبْتُمْ مَكَاتِيبَكُمْ لِأَصْحَابِكُمُ ٱلْيَوْمَ؟ ٢- نَعَمْ، كَتَبْنَاهَا وَوَضَعْنَاهَا عَلَى تِلْكَ ٱلْمَائِدَةِ ٱلْكَبِيرَةِ. ٣- طَلَبَ ٱلسَّائِلُ أَكْلًا (طَعَامًا) مِنِّي. ٤- فَتَحَتِ ٱلْخَادِمَةُ بَابَ ٱلْبَيْتِ فَدَخَلُوا (وَدَخَلُوا). ٥- هَلْ خَرَجْتَ لِلصَّيْدِ ٱلْيَوْمَ؟ لَا، مَا خَرَجْتُ لِلصَّيْدِ، ذَهَبْتُ إِلَى ٱلْمَدِينَةِ لِلسُّوقِ. ٦- (قَدْ) غَرَبَتِ ٱلشَّمْسُ وَطَلَعَ ٱلْقَمَرُ. ٧- دَخَلَ مُحَمَّدٌ وَٱبْنُهُ فِي ٱلْمَدِينَةِ وَخَرَجَا مِنْهَا بَعْدَ سَاعَةٍ. ٨- ضَرَبَنِي قَبْلَ دَقِيقَتَيْنِ. ٩- جَلَسَ ٱلرِّجَالُ وَشَرِبُوا شَايًا مَعَ ٱلشَّيْخِ. ١٠- رَجَعْنَا مِنَ ٱلصَّيْدِ مَعَ ٱلْوَزِيرِ، ثُمَّ حَضَرْنَا ٱجْتِمَاعَ ٱلْمَجْلِسِ. ١١- شَرِبُوا ٱلْقَهْوَةَ مَعَ ٱلنِّسَاءِ. ١٢- قَبِلْتُ ٱلضُّيُوفَ عِنْدِي وَزَوْجَتِي قَبِلَتِ ٱلضَّيْفَاتِ. ١٣- نَزَلْتُ عِنْدَ حَسَنٍ وَأَخِيهِ مُحَمَّدٍ. ١٤- هَلْ فَهِمْتَ قَوْلِي؟

18

١٥ـ قَالَ هٰذَا قَبْلَ سَاعَةٍ ، وَعَرَفْتُهُ مِنْ كُتُبِهِ . ١٦ـ لِمَاذَا
قَفَلْتِ الْبَابَ وَفَتَحْتِ الشُّبَّاكَ (اَلنَّافِذَةَ) ؟١٧ـ اَلرِّيحُ
مِنَ الشَّمَالِ الْيَوْمَ . ١٨ـ دَرَسْتَ هٰذَا الْمَوْضُوعَ قَبْلَ
شُهُورٍ (أَشْهُرٍ) . ١٩ـ رَكِبُوا حُصْنَهُمْ وَقَصَدُوا دِمَشْقَ
فَوَصَلُوا (وَوَصَلُوا) هُنَاكَ بَعْدَ يَوْمَيْنِ . ٢٠ـ ذَهَبَتِ
الْبَنَاتُ لِلْمَدْرَسَةِ وَطَلَبْنَ الْكُتُبَ الْجَدِيدَةَ .

Exercise 23

1. The women heard the news of the death of the prime minister, so they put on their black clothes, and mourned greatly. 2. And the sorrow of the merchants was great also. 3. Ali had taken me to the city, and I saw a light there in one of the king's castles. 4. Important news has reached us about the policy of the new government (*or* the new policy of the government). 5. Italy was one of the major (*or* great) powers. 6. We were sad when the enemy (*pl.*) imprisoned many of our soldiers a year ago (*lit.* before a year). 7. I had many fruits in my garden, including apples and dates.* 8. The university professor mentioned the important animals, including horses and sheep,* and he also mentioned fish(es).* 9. He said to them: "Why did you take my son

* The definite article is used in Arabic here, because the writer or speaker is not thinking indefinitely of *some* apples, dates, horses, sheep and fish, but of the whole species. This definite article of generalisation is used in English only with the singular, but not with the plural: *e.g.* we say "*The* horse is a noble animal", but "Horses are noble animals". In each case, we mean *all horses* or *the horse as a species.* Arabic, however, uses the definite article of generalisation with both singular and plural nouns.

Sentence 8 above could really be translated alternatively: "The university professor mentioned the important animals, including *the* horse and *the* sheep".

and beat him?" 10. The boys found (some) cloth in the street, and took it. 11. My mother put the sugar on the table. 12. This ministry had done that many years ago (or previously). 13. Your ministry is very weak now. 14. What goods (or merchandise) has that rich merchant? 15. He has cloths of all colours (or types). 16. Today, sugar is the most important of the goods of our country. 17. The ministers arrived, all of them, (and) entered the palace (or castle), and sat on their chairs, then the president (or chairman, or prime minister) arrived. 18. The new ministry (or cabinet) had an important meeting two days ago. 19. The Arabs asked for (or demanded) their camels, then mounted them. 20. The shaikh's (or old man's) camel was faster than all our horses (*lit.* our horses, all of them) yesterday.

Exercise 24

١- هَلْ وَصَلَكَ ٱلْخَبَرُ عَنْ مَوْتِ كَثِيرٍ مِنْ جُنُودِنَا ؟ ٢- لَا ،
وَحُزْنُنَا شَدِيدٌ ٱلْآنَ .٣- قَالَ رَئِيسُ ٱلْوُزَرَاءِ : لِهٰؤُلَاءِ
ٱلتُّجَّارِ بَضَائِعُ كَثِيرَةٌ مُهِمَّةٌ لِبِلَادِنَا .٤- وَذَكَرَ سِيَاسَةَ
ٱلْحُكُومَةِ ٱلْجَدِيدَةَ أَيْضاً . ٥- قَالَ عَلِيٌّ : كَانَتْ فَوَاكِهُ
كَثِيرَةٌ جَمِيلَةٌ فِي جُنَيْنَتِي لٰكِنْ دَخَلَهَا أَوْلَادُ ٱلْقَرْيَةِ
فِي ٱللَّيْلِ وَأَخَذُوهَا . ٦- حَزِنُوا لَمَّا سَمِعُوا قَوْلَهُ .٧-
قُمَاشُ هٰذِهِ ٱلثِّيَابِ قَدِيمٌ جِدًّا .هُوَ قُمَاشٌ جَيِّدٌ .
٨- وَجَدَ ٱلْجُنُودُ ٱلْأَعْدَاءَ فَأَسَرُوهُمْ . ٩- لَيْسَتِ ٱلنِّسَاءُ

20

ثِيَابَهُنَّ ٱلْبَيْضَاءَ لَمَّا رَجَعَ ٱلرِّجَالُ . ١٠- ٱلْقَاهِرَةُ أَكْبَرُ مَدِينَةٍ فِي ٱلشَّرْقِ ٱلْعَرَبِيِّ . ١١- كَانَتْ هٰذِهِ ٱلْغُرْفَانُ لِي مُنْذُ أَيَّامِ أَبِيكَ . ١٢- أَخَذَ كُلُّ تِلْمِيذٍ تُفَّاحَـــةً وَثَمَرَتَيْنِ مِنْ فَوَاكِهِ بُسْتَانِ ٱلْمَدْرَسَةِ . ١٣- مَاذَا عَمِلْتَ لِهٰذَا ٱلسَّمَكِ ؟ ١٤- رَكِبَ ٱلْجُنُودُ أَحْصِنَتَهُمْ لِلْقَلْعَـةِ فَأَخَذُوهَا وَأَسَرُوا ٱلسُّكَّانَ . ١٥- فَتَلُوا ٱلْكِبَارَ وَتَرَكُوا ٱلصِّغَارَ كُلَّهُمْ . ١٦- كَانَتْ أَنْوَارٌ مِنْ بَيْتِ صَدِيقِي . ١٧-عِنْدَ ذٰلِكَ ٱلتَّاجِرِ جَمِيعُ ٱلسُّكَّرِ فِي ٱلسُّوقِ . ١٨-كَانَتِ ٱلزَّوْجَاتُ (قَدْ) طَلَبْنَ عَمَلاً كَثِيرًا مِنْ خَادِمَاتِهِنَّ فَتَرَكَتْ هٰؤُلَاءِ ٱلطَّعَامَ عَلَى ٱلْمَائِدَةِ وَخَرَجْنَ . ١٩- قَدْ حَضَرْنَا جَمِيـعَ (كُلَّ) ٱجْتِمَاعَاتِ ٱلْمَجْلِسِ . ٢٠- كُنْتُمْ أَصْـدِقَاءَنَا (أَصْحَابَنَا) وَٱلْآنَ أَنْتُمْ أَعْدَاؤُنَا . *

Exercise 25

1. What will prevent you from that in the afternoon (*or* this afternoon)?   2. Will you carry a part of that or not?   3. The mother said to her small son: "What (thing) have you broken now?"   4. So the boy said: "I was playing in the room, and

* See pp. 114 ff of the Grammar.

21

something fell off the table". 5. The ministers will be in session (*lit.* sit) for a week, in accordance with the prime minister's (*or* president's, *or* chairman's) words. 6. The woman washed her clothes in the river in the morning. 7. I considered all the porters lazy (*lit.* the porters lazy, all of them). 8. Muḥammad was a great prophet. 9. The sunlight (*lit.* light of the sun) will be strong in the afternoon. 10. The pupils used to smoke at first, and that was a great burden to (*lit.* on) the teacher. 11. He assembled the army, and said to the soldiers: "God is greatest". 12. Will you do this work during the night or tomorrow? 13. We shall hear the news from Egypt in the evening. 14. The inhabitants are nice, and their ministers are among the best of people. 15. The women will enter their houses and live in them till the beginning of the new year. 16. When this boy grows up he will be one of the best of men. 17. The porters cut the ropes of their loads and lifted them off their donkeys. 18. After this work (*lit.* these works) your name will be honoured among your brothers and sisters. 19. This daughter of mine will have attended school lessons since the beginning of the year and will have studied the subject a great deal. Then why do you not listen to what she says? (*lit.* her speech). 20. When you reach the <u>shaikh</u>'s house, you will ask him for tea.

Exercise 26

١- نَحْنُ طُلَّابٌ وَنَطْلُبُ ٱلْعِلْمَ . ٢- فِى ٱلْبَدْءِ تَقْدِرُتِ ٱلنِّسَاهُ ضَوْءَ ٱلشَّمْسِ ، وَسَوْفَ * يَنْظُرْنَهُ أَيْضاً بَعْدَ ٱلظُّهْـرِ. ٣- سَيَحْمِلُ * ٱلْحَمَّالُونَ جَمِيعَ ٱلْأَحْمَالِ مِنَ ٱلْبَيْتِ لِلسَّيَّارَةِ

* The alternative usage of سَ or سَوْفَ for the future will not normally be indicated in this key.

(لِلْعَرَبِ) .٤- أَكُنْتُمْ تَجْمَعُونَ ٱلصَّنَادِيقَ فِي ٱلصَّبَاحِ أَمْ لَا؟

٥- يَكُونُ نَبِيءُ (نَبِيُّ) ٱللهِ (قَدْ) ذَهَبَ إِلَى مَكَّةَ غَدًا

فِي ٱلْمَسَاءِ .٦- سَوْفَ يَسْمَعُ ٱلنَّاسُ ٱلْأَخْبَارَ وَيَنْقُلُونَ

وُزَرَاءَهُمْ . ٧ - قَطَعَ عَلِيٌّ ٱلْحَبْلَ مِنْ يَدَيْ صَدِيقَيْهِ بِٱللَّيْلِ

فَكَسَرَا جُزْءًا مِنَ ٱلْحَائِطِ وَخَرَجَا مِنَ ٱلْقَلْعَةِ. ٨-يَكُونُ

هَذَا ٱلشَّيْءُ عَيْنًا كَبِيرًا عَلَيْنَا . ٩- هِيَ تَكُونُ فِي دِمَشْقَ

بَعْدَ أُسْبُوعَيْنِ . ١٠- كَانَتْ تَشْرَبُ دُخَانًا كَثِيرًا لَكِنْ

مَنَعَهَا أَبُوهَا قَبْلَ (مُنْذُ) سَنَةٍ .١١- لَنَا حُقُوقٌ كَثِيرَةٌ

قَدِيمَةٌ ، وَٱلْحُكُومَةُ تَعْرِفُهَا .١٢- كَانَ أَبِي يَدْفَعُ أَحْجَارًا

كَبِيرَةً مِنَ ٱلْأَرْضِ وَيَحْمِلُهَا مِنْ جُنَيْنَتِنَا لِجُنَيْنَةٍ حَسَنٍ.

١٣- يَغْسِلُ ٱلْوَلَدُ ٱلنَّظِيفُ وَجْهَهُ وَيَدَيْهِ كُلَّ يَوْمٍ صَبَاحًا

وَمَسَاءً .١٤- مَاذَا تَعْمَلُ ٱلْآنَ؟ هَلْ تَدْرُسُ دُرُوسَكَ؟

١٥- قَدْ كَسَرَ كُلَّ شَيْءٍ فِي ٱلْغُرْفَةِ .١٦- كَانَ ٱلْعَرَبُ كِرَامًا

وَكَانُوا يَسْكُنُونَ فِي ٱلصَّحْرَاءِ .١٧-كُنْتُ أَحْسِبُهُ

أَحْسَنَ مِنِّي فِي هَذَا ٱلْعَمَلِ . ١٨- بِنَاءً عَلَى قَوْلِ ٱلرَّئِيسِ

23

حَضَرْنَا الاِجْتِمَاعَ . ١٩- قَدْ كَبُرَ الْوَزِيرُ - فَهُوَ اَكْبَرُ
وَزِيرٍ فِي الْعَالَمِ الْعَرَبِيِّ الْيَوْمَ . ٢٠ - سَيَبْلُغُكَ الْخَبَرُ
غَدًا حِينَ تَكُونُ فِي الاِجْتِمَاعِ .

Exercise 27

1. The director (*or* governor, etc.) has asked you to go to
his house (*lit.* to attend).   2. I ordered the two of them to be
seated.   3. The merchant came to (*lit.* attended at) my
house to ask for the merchandise.   4. Did you open the
door for them to enter our house? I will open the door for
them at once.   5. The men went out to go hunting.   6. The
youth asked the man to allow him a clean room in which to
spend the (*lit.* his) night.   7. I opened the door to enter the
room.   8. The sultan's commands were that the governor
should return from his visit to Britain to do his duty in his
(own) country.   9. The man told these lies so as to be
famous throughout (*lit.* in the whole of) Europe.   10. The
king ordered his soldiers to cut the lazy watchman's bonds so
that he might return to his important work.   11. Workers
are asked not to leave their manual labour until the party
orders them to do so.   12. The chairman said in the committee: "One of the duties of newspapers is to write the
truth".   13. You shall not lie on your bed before my (very)
eyes!   14. The intelligent boy promised to do that which
was in God's Book and in the sayings (*sing. in the Arabic*) of
the Prophet.   15. White and black people have red blood in
their bodies.   16. The <u>sh</u>aikh sent his eldest (*lit.* old) son to
study (*lit.* seek learning) there.   17. The guest advanced
till he reached the castle (*or* palace) gate, then he asked the
soldier to open it.   18. What do you intend from this evil
(deed)?   19. I asked him about these matters yesterday, and

he asked for time to study them.   20. He told him to take
the oldest book in the library so that the learned might look
at it (*or* see it).

Exercise 28

١- بَعَثْتُ وَلَدًا مَعَهُ لِيَنْظُرَ مَا يَعْمَلُ . ٢- قَصَدَ مُحَمَّدٌ

وَخَادِمُهُ أَنْ يَذْهَبَا إِلَى ٱلسُّوقِ . ٣- سَوْفَ أَرْجِعُ لِلْبَيْتِ

لِأَنْظُرَ مَا تَعْمَلُ . ٤- أَمَرْتُ ٱلْخَادِمَ أَنْ يَحْضُرَ أَمَامِي . ٥-

وَعَدْتُهُ بِأَنْ (رَأَنْ) يَكُونَ ذَلِكَ سِرًّا بَيْنِي وَبَيْنَهُ.   ٦-

أَتَسْمَحُ لِي بِأَنْ أَتْرُكَ هَذِهِ ٱلْأَشْيَاءَ عِنْدَكَ حَتَّى ٱلْمَسَاءِ؟

٧- قَدْ أَمَرَ ٱلْمُعَلِّمُ أَنْ تَصْرِفُوا ٱلْيَوْمَ (ٱلنَّهَارَ) كُلَّـهُ

فِي ٱلْفَصْلِ لِتَعْمَلُوا مَا طَلَبَ مِنْكُمْ أَمْسِ. ٨- ٱلْمَطْلُوبُ مِنَ

ٱلْفِئَرَانِ أَنْ يَتْرُكُوا أَعْمَالَهُمْ لِيَحْضُرُوا ٱجْتِمَاعًا لِحِزْبِ

ٱلْعُمَّالِ لَكَيْ يَسْمَعُوا خَبَرَ زِيَارَةِ ٱلرَّئِيسِ لِبِرِيطَانِيَـا

وَإِيطَالِيَا . ٩- قَدِمَ ٱلسَّفِينُ مِنْ أُورُبَّا قَبْلَ شَهْرَيْـنِ

لِيَسْأَلَ عَنْ حَقِيقَةِ ٱلْأَمْنِ. ١٠ عَلَيْكَ (لَكَ) أَنْ تَعْمَلَ

(تَفْعَلَ) وَاجِبَكَ . ١١- لِلرَّجُلِ ٱلْعَاقِلِ أَنْ يَعْرِفَ ٱلْحَقَائِقَ

مِنَ ٱلْأَكْذَابِ فِي ٱلْجَرَائِدِ . ١٢- طَلَبَ ٱلرِّجَالُ مِنْ زَوْجَاتِهِمْ

أَنْ يَكُنَّ فِي بُيُوتِهِنَّ بَعْدَ الظُّهْرِ، وَكَانَ ذٰلِكَ صَعْبًا عَلَيْهِنَّ . ١٣- لِمَاذَا تَرْقُدُ عَلَى فِرَاشِكَ؟ هَلْ جِسْمُكَ ضَعِيفٌ أَمْ أَنْتَ كَسْلَانُ؟ ١٤- حَضَرَ الْمُدِيرُ وَمُدِيرُ الْأَشْغَالِ اجْتِمَاعَ اللَّجْنَةِ لِيَسْمَعَا أَوَامِرَ الْحُكُومَةِ . ١٥- لِهٰذِهِ التُّفَّاحِ لَوْنُ الدَّمِ، هِيَ مِنْ أَجْمَلِ الْفَوَاكِهِ فِي بُسْتَانِكَ . ١٦- فَتَحُوا شَبَابِيكَ (نَوَافِذَ) الْغُرْفَةِ (الْحُجْرَةِ) حَتَّى يَنْظُرَ أَقْرِبَاؤُهُمُ الشَّمْسَ صَبَاحًا (فِي الصَّبَاحِ) . ١٧- ضَوْءُ الْقَمَرِ جَمِيلٌ اللَّيْلَةَ . ١٨- أَمَرَ الْمُدِيرُ رِجَالَهُ بِأَنْ (رَأَنْ) يَقْطَعُوا قُيُودَ حَسَنٍ لِأَنْ يَرْجِعَ لِأُمِّهِ . ١٩- قَالُوا لِلْوَلَدَيْنِ أَنْ يَفْتَحَا الْبَابَ حَتَّى تَدْخُلَ النِّسَاءُ . ٢٠- لَنْ تَكْسِرَ شَيْئًا فِي هٰذَا الْبَيْتِ .

Exercise 29

1. The minister did not permit any man (*lit.* did not permit a man) to sit beside him.   2. Don't leave your friend in need.   3. The men recognised (*lit.* knew) him, and did not prevent him from entering, so he entered.   4. Her heart found no pleasure (*lit.* did not rejoice) in anything.   5. Girl, do not open the door to strangers.   6. Don't be sad, boys! 7. We are tired, so let us sit down for a minute in this place.

26

8. They could not return to town (*or* to the city).   9. The
boy saw a house, and there was no other in that place.
10. God said "Let there be light" and there was light.
11. Let our journey to our home-country be next month
(*lit.* in the coming month), but don't lie in this way, clerk!
12. An Arab writer investigated the state of Arabia, and said
in one of his articles in today's paper: "There are many poor
(people) and few rich".   13. The services of this scholar
have been excellent.   14. The sun is strong here, so let us
dismount here in this very shady spot.   15. Some newspapers have published that news in the name of the prime
minister.   16. Do not enter the Egyptian embassy (*lit.* the
house of the embassy of Egypt) after this, you liar.   17. Let
me be your friend.   18. Do not on any account publish this
article.   19. The government has ordered him to publish
the truth (the facts).   20. Will you go to the market,
daughter.*

Exercise 30

١- مَا عَرَفْتُ ٱلْأَمْرَ وَلَمْ أَفْهَمْهُ . ٢- يَا أَوْلَادُ، لَاتَفْتَحُوا

ٱلْبَابَ . يَا بِنْتُ، لَا تَكْذِبِى . ٣- كَانَ ٱلتَّلَامِيذُ كَسَالَى

وَمَا عَمِلُوا (وَلَمْ يَعْمَلُوا**) وَاجِبَهُمْ . ٤- سَمِعُوا قَوْلَكَ

وَلَمْ يَفْهَمُوهُ . ٥- لَا تَتْرُكْ أَصْدِقَاءَكَ فِى ٱلصِّينِ . ٦- لَا

تَمْنَعْنِى مِنَ ٱلذَّهَابِ . ٧- لِنَشْرَبِ ٱلْقَهْوَةَ . ٨- لَمْ يَقْدِرِ

* The jussive is used here as a polite command.

** As مَا plus the *perfect* is the equivalent of لَمْ plus the *jussive*, it is
not considered necessary to indicate the alternative translations
throughout the key.

ٱلْأَبُ وَٱبْنُهُ أَنْ يَرْجِعَا إِلَى بَيْتِهِمَا . ٩- لِأَكُنْ بِجَانِبِكَ بَيْنَ هَؤُلَاءِ ٱلنَّاسِ ٱلْغُرَبَاءِ فِي هَذَا ٱلْمَكَانِ ٱلْغَرِيبِ . ١٠- يَا مُحَمَّدُ ، قُلْتُ لِحَسَنٍ أَنْ يَدْخُلَ لَكِنْ دَخَلَ غَيْرُهُ . ١١- فِي ٱلْأُسْبُوعِ ٱلْقَادِمِ يَقْدَمُ عَالِمٌ مَشْهُورٌ إِلَى ٱلسِّفَارَةِ لِيَبْحَثَ فِي حَالِ ٱلْمَدَارِسِ فِي وَطَنِنَا . ١٢- لَا يَعْمَلَنَّ (يَعْمَلَنْ) (لَنْ يَعْمَلَ or) ٱلْكَتَبَةُ ٱلْفُقَرَاءُ كُلَّ يَوْمٍ فِي خِدْمَةِ هَذِهِ ٱلْحُكُومَةِ . ١٣- لِتَنْشُرِ ٱلْجَرَائِدُ ٱلْأَخْبَارَ ٱلطَّيِّبَةَ حَتَّى يَعْرِفَهَا ٱلنَّاسُ حَالاً . ١٤- أَمَرْتُهُ بِأَنْ يَذْهَبَ لَكِنْ لَمْ يَذْهَبْ . ١٥- مَالِطَةُ (مَالْطَا) جَزِيرَةٌ صَغِيرَةٌ وَٱلسَّفَرُ إِلَيْهَا جَمِيلٌ جِدًّا . ١٦- كَتَبَ بَعْضُ ٱلْكُتَّابِ (كَاتِبٌ مِنَ ٱلْكُتَّابِ) مَقَالَةً جَيِّدَةً فِي هَذَا ٱلْمَوْضُوعِ . ١٧- لَا تَعْمَلْ بِهَذِهِ ٱلطَّرِيقَةِ يَا عَامِلُ . ١٨- لِتَكُنْ بَغْدَادُ أَجْمَلَ مَدِينَةٍ تَحْتَ ٱلشَّمْسِ يَا عُمَّالُ، فَعَلَيْكُمْ أَنْ تَعْمَلُوا وَاجِبَاتِكُمْ. ١٩- قَدْ تَرَكَ بِلَادَنَا ، فَلَا يَرْجِعْ (يَرْجِعَنَّ) . ٢٠- هَذِهِ هِيَ ٱلْحَقِيقَةُ، فَلْتَذْكُرْهَا فِي قَوْلِهَا .

Exercise 31

1. Open the door, mother. 2. Do not come in, boys. 3. Tell the truth, and do not lie, pupils. 4. Keep silent, pupil, and sit in your place. 5. Open the house door, 'Abdullāh. 6. Men, prevent them from entering in to us. 7. Look, madam, what you have done. 8. They found a woman seated (sitting) in a small room. 9. Follow the religion of Islam, O you unbelievers. 10. Girl, listen to the words of the witnesses in court. 11. I found the thief near the well with a Turkish tribe. 12. It is very cold in the mountains of Turkey. 13. Madam (*or* lady), don't do that. 14. We are in the middle of the cold part of Turkey. 15. They went to Beirut by land, and we went by sea. 16. Don't be mean, my son. 17. We saw the bodies of the dead in the desert when we went to Damascus. 18. Be truthful, 'Abdullāh, for that is an important thing in the religion of Islam. 19. We are following the army to battle. 20. Don't be liars.

Exercise 32

١- يَا أَوْلَادُ ، ٱنْظُرُوا مَا فَعَلْتُمْ (عَمِلْتُمْ) . ٢- يَا صَدِيقُ
ٱدْخُلْ وَٱجْلِسْ بِجَانِبِي . ٣- يَا تِلْمِيذُ (أَيُّهَا ٱلتِّلْمِيذُ)
ٱفْتَحْ بَابَ ٱلْغُرْفَةِ . ٤- كُنْتُ أَذْهَبُ (ذَاهِبًا) إِلَى
ٱلْمَدِينَةِ . ٥- أَيْنَ يَسْكُنُ ٱلسَّيِّدُ حَسَنٌ ؟ ٦-هُوَ سَاكِنٌ
(يَسْكُنُ) فِي وَسْطِ ٱلْمَدِينَةِ . ٧- كُنْتُ أَكْتُبُ (كَاتِبًا)
مَكْتُوبًا ، فَدَخَلَ صَدِيقُنَا . ٨- لَا تَمْنَعْنِي مِنَ ٱلدُّخُولِ
عَلَيْكَ . ٩- هُمْ سَرَقَةٌ مَشْهُورُونَ (مَشَاهِيرُ) وَقَـــدْ

29

١٠- نَظَرْتُهُمْ فِي ٱلْمَحْكَمَةِ لَمَّا كُنْتُ شَاهِدًا . يَا أَيَّتُهَا ٱلسَّيِّدَةُ ، لَا تَكُونِي مِنَ ٱلْكَافِرَاتِ ؛ اِتْبَعِي دِينَ ٱلْإِسْلَامِ . ١١- رَجَعَ ٱلتُّرْكِيُّ ٱلْبَخِيلُ لِوَطَنِهِ بَرًّا (بِٱلْبَرِّ) . ١٢- قَـالَ ٱلسُّلْطَانُ لِلْعَرَبِ: اُسْكُنُوا يَا أَيُّهَا ٱلظُّرَفَاءُ . ١٣- أَصْدُقْنَ يَا نِسَاءُ ! أَذَهَبَ رِجَالُ ٱلْقَرْيَةِ لِلْقِتَالِ أَمْ لَا ؟ ١٤- كَانَ جِسْمُ (بَدَنُ) ٱلرَّجُلِ ٱلْمَيِّتِ بَارِدًا جِدًّا . ١٥- ٱلْبَرْدُ شَدِيدٌ فِي جِبَالِ تُرْكِيَّا . ١٦- كَانَ ٱلْعَرَبُ يَرْكَبُونَ (رَاكِبِينَ) جِمَالَهُمْ إِلَى ٱلْبِئْرِ ٱلْقَرِيبَةِ . ١٧- فِي مَكَاتِبِ ٱلْحُكُومَـةِ بِٱلْقَاهِرَةِ (فِي ٱلْقَاهِرَةِ) كَتَبَةٌ كَثِيرُونَ . ١٨- اِذْهَبُوا إِلَى ٱلْمَدْرَسَةِ يَا أَوْلَادُ وَٱدْرُسُوا دُرُوسَكُمْ . ١٩- قَدْ وَصَلَ طَلَبَةُ (طُلَّابُ) دِمَشْقَ فِي (إِلَى) ٱلْقَاهِرَةِ لِٱجْتِمَاعٍ مُهِمٍّ مَعَ إِخْوَانِهِمِ ٱلْمِصْرِيِّينَ . ٢٠- اُتْرُكْ هَذَا ٱلْعَمَلَ لِلنِّسَاءِ

Exercise 33

1. Ḥasan's name was mentioned for his bravery, and because he was among the wounded. 2. Zaid is the striker, and

'Umar the struck (*in more idiomatic English*, Zaid is the assailant and 'Umar the victim). 3. We have learned from history books and the life of the Prophet that his army was defeated that (*lit*. this) day, but it (*or* he) defeated his (*or* its) foes later (*lit*. after that). 4. News (has) reached us from his honour the deputy that he is (*or* was) busy. 5. We wrote a letter to him two months ago, and we have heard no news of him. Perhaps he is angry with us (*lit*. has become angry with us). 6. Tonight there is great light in the sky from those stars. 7. This famous doctor said that the fear of death is the greatest danger to the invalid (*or* patient, sick man). 8. The Jew was ordered to advance to the minister and bring with him costly presents. 9. We belong to God, and to him we shall return. 10. This historian is (well-) known among scholars. 11. The soldier's sword broke, so the prisoners' joy increased (*or* became great). 12. We have heard from today's paper that the loss of this rich merchant is considerable (*lit*..very great). 13. Wood is an important material. 14. The girl did not enter the house because the key was lost. 15. This period is long for your small job. 16. It is written (*lit*. was written) in history that the army crossed the river, and reached Baghdad two hours later. 17. Aḥmad, what have you studied about the many peoples of the world? You are *indeed ignorant. 18. Go back to your place, girl, perhaps you will be sensible after this. 19. He told the women to mount (*or* ride), so they mounted (*or* rode) their donkeys. 20. Kill your enemies, soldiers, that is *surely one of your duties.

---

* In sentences 17 and 20, the particle اِنَّ is translated as "indeed" and "surely". Although this particle is frequently not translated at all, there may be contexts in which it appears to give some stress – particularly in modern Arabic. The translator must, therefore, use his own judgment on whether to introduce some stress word such as "indeed" and "surely" as above. Experience will make this decision easier.

١- فُتِحَتْ أَبْوَابُ ٱلْبَيْتِ وَقُبِلَتِ ٱلْهَدَايَا بِسُرُورٍ بِالسُّرُورِ.

٢- مَا عَرَفْتُ أَنَّكَ مَشْغُولٌ ٱلْيَوْمَ. ٣- أَعْرِفُ أَنَّ ٱلْعَرَبَ هُمُ

ٱلْغَالِبُونَ وَٱلْأَعْدَاءَ ٱلْمَغْلُوبُونَ. ٤- ٱلرِّجَالُ ٱلْمَذْكُورُونَ مِنْ

أَصْدِقَائِي. ٥- ذُكِرَتْ شَجَاعَتُهُ فِي كُتُبِ ٱلتَّأْرِيخِ. ٦- قُتِلَ

بِالسَّيْفِ لِأَنَّ ٱلْمَجَانِينَ غَضِبُوا عَلَيْهِ. ٧- قَدْ كُنْتَ هُنَا

مُدَّةً طَوِيلَةً، فَلَعَلَّكَ تَذْهَبُ ٱلْآنَ. ٨- ٱلتُّرَّابُ ٱلْمَرْضَى

حَضَرُوا هٰذَا ٱلِٱجْتِمَاعَ لِأَنَّ ٱلْأُمَّةَ طَلَبَتْ ذٰلِكَ مِنْهُمْ.

٩- إِنَّ ٱلشَّجَاعَةَ خَيْرٌ مِنَ ٱلْخَوْفِ. ١٠- قَالَ إِنَّ كُلَّ ٱلْخَشَبِ

قَدْ وُضِعَ عَلَى ٱلنَّارِ. ١١- اُنْظُرْ سِيَرَ ٱلرِّجَالِ ٱلْعِظَامِ فِي

كُتُبِ ٱلْمُوَرِّخِينَ. ١٢- عَبَرَ جُنُودٌ كَثِيرُونَ ٱلنَّهْرَ لٰكِنَّ ٱلْجَوَارِيحَ

مَا قَدَرُوا (عَلَى) أَنْ يَتْرُكُوا مَوَاضِعَهُمْ فَقُتِلُوا. ١٣- إِنَّ فِي

ٱلنُّجُومِ مَوَادَّ كَثِيرَةً نَفِيسَةً. ١٤- فَقَدْ حَضَرَ ٱلتَّائِبُ

مِفْتَاحَ سَيَّارَتِهِ فَرَجَعَ إِلَى بَيْتِهِ فِي سَيَّارَةِ صَدِيقِهِ ٱلْقَدِيمَةِ.

١٥- سَمِعْتُ أَنَّ خَسَارَاتِ التُّجَّارِ كَانَتْ كَثِيرَةً جِدًّا فِي هٰذِهِ السَّنَةِ . ١٦- سَبَبُ (إِنَّ سَبَبَ) ذٰلِكَ خَطَرُ الْحَرْبِ . ١٧- إِنَّ الْيَهُودَ أُمَّةٌ قَدِيمَةٌ جِدًّا فِي تَأْرِيخِ الْعَالَمِ . ١٨- إِنَّ فِي قُلُوبِكُمْ خَوْفَ اللّٰهِ . فَلْيَنْتَحْ لَكُمْ أَبْوَابَ السَّمٰوَاتِ . ١٩- يَا حَسَنُ أَنْتَ (إِنَّكَ) رَجُلٌ عَظِيمُ الْيَوْمَ ، وَقَبْلَ سَنَةٍ كُنْتَ مِنَ الْفُقَرَاءِ . ٢٠- قَالَ الْمُعَلِّمُ إِنَّ سُلَيْمَانَ كَانَ مَلِكَ الْيَهُودِ .

Exercise 35

1. This stone is (fixed) firm(ly) in the wall, and it is very heavy. 2. I have a bad headache, boy. 3. The international committee's new session will be in Egypt. 4. And it will be attended by some foreigners. 5. The reason and subject of the meeting is freedom. 6. I wrote to Husain in the spring, and his reply reached me in the autumn. 7. His body was found in his neighbour's house, and he was dead, and his murderer is unknown. 8. They left the gates of the city without a guard, because they had all gone to the election. 9. The beauty of the Lebanon in summer is well-known among foreigners, but it is much more beautiful in winter. 10. The rain was light, and especially in spring. 11. I have paid the two pounds from my own private money. 12. Consequently I am angry with you. 13. Where are the two books by (*lit.* of) this great author, in the library? 14. I shut the windows, and sat by the feeble fire. 15. The young boy was left without father or mother. 16. How many

33

dirhems have you ? 17. Don't be a liar, be upright. 18. The biography of the Prophet is very beneficial to Muslims. 19. Ask your friend to cross the road, and go to the baker's shop in the old market. 20. It is your duty to listen to what relatives say (*lit.* the speech of the relatives).

Exercise 36

١- اَلْاِنْتِخَابَاتُ قَرِيبَةٌ وَأَنَا بِدُونِ سَيَّارَتِي . ٢- اِنْفِعِ الدِّرْهَمَيْنِ وَأَرْجِعْ إِلَى بَيْتِكَ أَيُّهَا السَّارِقُ ! ٣- هٰذَا هُوَكِتَابِي اَلْمَخْصُوصُ فَلَا تَذْهَبْ بِهِ . ٤- اَلْاِجْتِمَاعَاتُ اَلدُّوَلِيَّةُ مُهِمَّةٌ وَخُصُوصًا فِي مُدَّةِ اَلْخَطَرِ هٰذِهِ . ٥- حُسَيْنٌ أَبُوحَسَنٍ وَأَخُو مُحَمَّدٍ، وَهُوَ أَطْوَلُ رَجُلٍ فِي اَلْحُجْرَةِ وَأَجَدُّ نَائِبٍ فِي لُبْنَانَ . ٦- سَمِعْتُ أَنَّ لَكَ وَجَعًا فِي رَأْسِكَ (فِي اَلرَّأْسِ) . ٧- لِمَاذَا لَا تَطْلُبُ اَلطَّبِيبَ ؟ ٨- قَالَ اَلْأَجْنَبِيُّ لِلْبِنْتِ إِنَّهُ قَدْ سَمِعَ عَنْ جَمَالِهَا مِنْ جَارِهِ . ٩- هٰذَا كِتَابٌ تَمْثِيلٌ ـ فَذٰلِكَ اَلْخَفِيفُ أَحْسَنُ لِوَلَدٍ صَغِيرٍ . ١٠- كَانَتِ اَلْحُرِّيَّةُ مَجْهُولَةً بَيْنَ اَلْمِصْرِيَّيْنِ قَبْلَ أَيَّامِ اَلْإِسْلَامِ . ١١- مَا هُوَ جَوَابُكَ إِلَى كَلِمَاتِ اَلْحَارِسِ ؟ ١٢- نَظَرْتُ حُسَيْنًا فِي اَلرَّبِيعِ ، ثُمَّ لَمْ أَنْظُرْهُ حَتَّى اَلسَّنَةِ

34

الْجَدِيدَةِ . ١٣- اَلصَّيْفُ خَيْرٌ مِنَ الشِّتَاءِ فِي بِلَادِنَا، لٰكِنَّ

الْخَرِيفَ أَحْسَنُ فَصْلٍ . ١٤- هٰذِهِ الْجَلْسَةُ (إِنَّ هٰـذِهِ

الْجَلْسَةَ) مُهِمَّةٌ جِدًّا لِلْعَرَبِ . ١٥- أَتَكُونُ فِي الْمَدْرَسَـةِ

هٰذَا الْمَسَاءَ بَعْدَ الدُّرُوسِ؟ ١٦- سَأَلْتُكَ (طَلَبْتُ مِنْكَ) أَلَّا

(أَنْ لَا) تَرْجِعَ بِدُونِ أُخْتِكَ . فَأَيْنَ هِيَ؟ ١٧- لِتَذْهَبْ إِلَى بَيْتِ

جَدَّتِهَا . ١٨- أَنْتَ شَرٌّ مِنْهُ . ١٩- (قَدْ) ضُرِبَ الْوَزِيرُ فِي

الشَّوَارِعِ وَضَارِبُوهُ مَجْهُولُونَ . ٢٠- إِسْأَلِ الْمَسَاجِينَ (اَطْلُبْ

مِنَ الْمَسَاجِينِ)، لَعَلَّهُمْ يَعْرِفُونَ .

Exercise 37

1. I told him to send an inspector to consult the Bedouins.
2. Slaughter the enemies, soldiers. 3. The father said to
his small daughter: "Kiss your mother". 4. The ministry's
inspectors witnessed the work of the boys from a distance.
5. The men searched that vicinity, and after the search they
returned. 6. The shaikh ordered them to go at once to give
(the) good news to the prince (or emir). 7. Zaid asked that
they should inform his father that he had found his son, and
would be home tomorrow (or next day). 8. The shaikh
learned (or knew, got to know) that his guest had mixed with
the bedouins. 9. "Man proposes, but God disposes"
(Proverb). 10. We will send him someone to inform him of
that. 11. Inform us of your name. (or Tell us your name).
12. I greeted my father in the Arab manner, that is: "Peace

(be) on you". 13. It is your duty to believe and defend your friends. 14. This clerk does his work well in the office, and treats his fellows (*lit.* brothers) kindly. Thus he has become the best man in the office. His place there is like that of *a father in the home or a king in his (*lit.* the) country. 15. You (*pl.*) have travelled to the furthest horizons of the world, because you are fond of travel. 16. I saw the army of the enemy round the town, so I entered the ruler's (*or* governor's) fortress and informed him of that but he interrupted me (*lit.* cut off my speech). 17. Then the enemy attacked the town during the night, and captured it without a struggle (*lit.* fight). 18. On that dark day, the sentry brought in a soldier, and the latter informed the king that his mother had been killed in the neighbouring city. 19. Bring coffee (*or* the coffee), women. 20. The man asked the shopkeeper to bind the book.

Exercise 38

١- يَا خَادِمُ قَدِّمْ لَنَا قَهْوَةً جَدِيدَةً حَالاً مِنَ ٱلْمَطْبَخِ. ٢-
أَمَرَهُمُ ٱلْوَزِيرُ أَنْ (بِأَنْ) يُحْضِرُوا ٱلسَّارِقَ. ٣- أَمَرْتُهُمْ أَنْ يُخْبِرُوا
أَصْدِقَاءَهُمْ عَنْ ذَلِكَ لَكِنَّهُمْ لَمْ يُصَدِّقُونِي .٤- ٱلْإِنْسَانُ يُدَبِّرُ
وَٱللّٰهُ يُقَدِّرُ. ٥- أَرْسِلْ ذَلِكَ ٱلرَّجُلَ إِلَيَّ لِكَيْ أُرَاقِبَ عَمَلَهُ،
فَقَدْ خَالَفَ أَوَامِرِي مَرَّاتٍ كَثِيرَةً. ٦- أَدْخِلِ ٱلطَّبِيبَ لِكَيْ
نُشَاوِرَهُ عَنْ (فِي) حَالَةِ ٱلْأَمِيرِ. ٧- يُبَشِّرُكُمُ ٱللّٰهُ بِٱبْنٍ ٱسْمُهُ

---

* Arabic must repeat the word "place" (مكان), as it cannot say "that of" literally.

The Arabic says "*the* father in the home" and "*the* king in *the* country": the changes above are more idiomatic in English.

36

يَسُوعُ . ٨- اَللَّهَاجَمَةُ خَيْرُ طَرِيقَةِ الدِّفَاعِ . ٩- لَا تُخَالِطِ النَّاسَ فِي الْبَيْتِ المُجَاوِرِ . ١٠- سَافَرَ مُفَتِّشُو الحُكُومَةِ إِلَى الْقَرْيَةِ وَسَلَّمُوا عَلَى الشَّيْخِ فَشَاهَدُوا سِبَاقَاتِ الخَيْلِ، ثُمَّ فَتَّشُوا الْبُيُوتَ الْجَدِيدَةَ . ١١- نَظَرْنَا الْبَدْوَ حَوْلَ الْبِئْرِ عَنْ بُعْدٍ أَثْنَاءَ (فِي أَثْنَاءِ) السَّفَرِ . ١٢- قَبَّلَ يَدَيْهَا وَأَخْبَرَهَا أَنَّهُ كَانَ (قَدْ) أَصْبَحَ رَئِيسَ الْوُزَرَاءِ . ١٣- يُغْرِمُونَ بِالسَّفَرِ . ١٤- سَأُعْلِمُكَ (سَأُخْبِرُكَ) أَثْنَاءَ الشَّهْرِ الْمُقْبِلِ . ١٥- كَانَ كَبِيرًا كَأَبِيهِ لَكِنَّ أُخْتَهُ كَانَت صَغِيرَةً كَأُمِّهَا . ١٦- كَانَ يُكَلِّمُ (مُكَلِّمًا) زَوْجَتَهُ لَكِنْ قَاطَعَتْهُ . ١٧- كَانَ الْأُفُقُ مُظْلِمًا لَكِنَّ الْبَدَوِيَّ رَكِبَ جَمَلَهُ وَتَرَكَ الْقَرْيَةَ . ١٨- أَحْسَنَ ابْنِي دُرُوسَهُ وَعَامَلَهُ مُعَلِّمُهُ بِلُطْفٍ . ١٩- أَيْنَ السَّلَامُ فِي عَالَمِنَا هَذَا؟ ٢٠- هُمْ مُفَتِّشُو الزِّرَاعَةِ الجُدُدُ .

Exercise 39

1. Do you speak Arabic (*lit.* the Arabic language)? Yes, sir, I speak it a little.   2. The prince and his brother sat speaking about these matters.   3. When the men heard that, they all advanced to his direction (*or* went over to his side).   4. Do you remember what I commanded you, maid?   5. We were

37

surprised at the strength of the enemy, and the severity of the fighting on that famous day. 6. The child laughed at his grandfather for his slowness when he crossed the street. 7. Co-operation with you is an important thing, and we are honoured by it. 8. Do not fight each other, friends, but make a show of agreeing together. 9. The Arab and the Englishman parted, and did not meet until the present time (*or* this time). 10. I am grateful to you, because you have taught me much of your difficult language. 11. A (*lit.* the) long arm is more important than a fine weapon to the strong soldier. 12. They followed the tracks of their brave enemies, then they parted afterwards. 13. My father said: "That is how matters stand (*lit.* the matter is like that), so don't expect to find me (*lit.* don't expect my presence) among your approvers". 14. We left them talking (*or* conversing). 15. Is it my duty to become a Christian because you are my wife, and you have become a Christian? 16. I reminded him but he did not remember. 17. Do not co-operate with that proud man. 18. How many guests are we expecting tonight? 19. It is anticipated that the king will go to Mecca. 20. We will receive (*or* take delivery of) the goods tomorrow.

Exercise 40

١- تَحَادَثْنَا عَنْ هٰذَا ٱلْأَمْرِ أَمْسِ صَبَاحًا وَلٰكِنَّنَا لَـمْ نَتَوَافَقْ . ٢- تَنَاتَلَ ٱلْمُسْلِمُونَ وَٱلنَّصَارَى قَبْلَ مُدَّةٍ طَوِيلَةٍ (مُنْذُ زَمَنٍ طَوِيلٍ) لٰكِنْ يَتَوَافَقُونَ ٱلْيَوْمَ فِى أُمُورٍ (أَشْيَاءَ) كَثِيرَةٍ . ٣- كَانَ ٱلْعُلَمَاءُ يَتَحَادَثُونَ عَنْ آثَارِ مِصْرَ . ٤- نَتَوَقَّعُ

تَقَدُّمُ ٱلْأَعْدَاءِ مِنْ هٰذِهِ ٱلْجِهَةِ. ٥- كَانَ ٱلْأَطْفَالُ مُتَشَكِّرِينَ لِيَدَّتِهِمْ فَقَبَّلُوهَا؛ وَتَعَجَّبْتُ مِنْ ذٰلِكَ. ٦-تَذَكَّرْتُ أَنَّهُمْ كَانُوا يَضْحَكُونَ عَلَيْهَا. ٧- لِنَتَرَافَقْ وَتَعَاوَنْ، فَلْتَتَعَلَّمْ عَمَلَنَا ٱلْجَدِيدَ ٱلْمُهِمَّ وَنَكُنْ أَقْوِيَاءَ فِي كُلِّ شَيْءٍ. ٨-كَذٰلِكَ لِتَتَبَّعْ طَرِيقَ ٱلْوَاجِبِ. ٩- تَقَاتَلَ زَيْدٌ وَحَسَنٌ بِشِدَّةٍ لٰكِنِ ٱنْكَسَرَتْ ذِرَاعُ حَسَنٍ فَوَقَعَ سَيْفُهُ عَلَى ٱلْأَرْضِ. ١٠- ٱلْقُوَّةُ أَهَمُّ مِنَ ٱلْأَسْلِحَةِ لِلشُّجَاعِ. ١١- تَفَارَقَ ٱلْمُسَافِرُونَ فِي ٱلْبَادِيَةِ وَقَتَلَهُمُ ٱلْبَدْوُ. ١٢- لَا أَفْهَمُكَ، تَكَلَّمِ (ٱللُّغَةَ) ٱلْعَرَبِيَّةَ. ١٣- أَنَا أَجْنَبِيٌّ، هَلْ تَقْدِرُ أَنْ تَتَمَهَّلَ فِي كَلَامِكَ، لَعَلِّي أَفْهَمُكَ! ١٤- تَتَجَاهَلُ أَيُّهَا ٱلسَّيِّدُ، تَعْرِفُ لُغَتَنَا. ١٥-تَقَابَلْنَا فِي دِمَشْقَ قَبْلَ سَنَتَيْنِ. ١٦- تَعَجَّبَ ٱلْمَلِكُ مِنْ شَجَاعَةِ جُنُودِهِ ٱلصِّغَارِ. ١٧- أَذْهَبُ إِلَى ٱلْجَامِعَةِ لِأُقَابِلَ أُسْتَاذًا (مِنَ ٱلْأَسَاتِذَةِ) ١٨- تَعَاوَنَّا أَثْنَاءَ ٱلْحَرْبِ ثُمَّ تَفَارَقْنَا بَعْدَهَا. ١٩- كَانَ ٱلْعَالِمُ يَتَجَاهَلُ فَلَمْ يَسْمَعِ ٱلنَّاسُ كَلِمَاتِهِ. ٢٠- كَانَ مِنَ

ٱلْمُتَوَقَّعِ أَنْ تَكُونَ ٱلْجَلْسَةُ طَوِيلَةً ، لِأَنَّ ٱلْمَوْضُوعَ صَعْبٌ *

وَمُهِمٌّ .

Exercise 41

1. We have (or had) been pleased at the discovery of this
money in the garden.   2. A car overturned in a main street,
and I think that two of the passengers have been taken (lit.
carried) to (the) hospital.   3. Why were you defeated? You
are many and the enemy are few in numbers.   4. The
(maid-)servant said: "Sir (or master), the cup broke and I
didn't break it".   5. A meeting was held yesterday between
the ambassadors of Britain, France and Germany, and after
an hour, the French ambassador went away.   6. Think of
this matter a long time.   7. I think that the political disturbance was/is caused by (lit. it's cause was/is) the lack of
liberty.   8. Where is the respect for fathers and mothers in
society today?   9. Turn to me, boy. How are you working?
10. This sort of work (deed) is not possible in Arab society.
11. When he approached us, we were waiting for him.
12. Recently the government has recognised the rights of
(the) youth.   13. Divide the apples in two.   14. Britain
was victorious over Germany and Italy in the late war.
15. We waited, and (lo and behold!) there was an Egyptian
soldier approaching us.   16. We have sharp (lit. cutting)
swords, so don't come near us.   17. I went on foot while my
wife rode my camel.   18. I write this letter with all respect.
19. The boys are absent, so let us go off and return in the
afternoon.   20. Think before you act! (lit. thought before
action!).

---

* There is no need to translate the word "was" after "the subject"
(الموضوع) because the past has already been established at the beginning
of the sentence.

١- اِنْتَصَرَ حِزْبُ الْعُمَّالِ فِي الاِنْتِخَابَاتِ الأَخِيرَةِ . ٢- كَمْ سَاعَةً

أَنْتَ فِي اِنْتِظَارِنَا ؟- ٣- اِلْتَفَتُّ إِلَيْهِ بِاحْتِرَامٍ ، وَسَلَّمْتُ عَلَيْهِ ،

فَانْصَرَفْتُ . ٤- سَوْفَ تَنْبَسِطُونَ (تَنْبَسِطُ) مِنْ أَقْسَامِكُمْ

(أَقْسَامِكَ) الْكَبِيرَةِ. ٥- قُلْتُ لِلسَّاسَةِ أَخِيرًا أَنْ يَعْتَرِفُوا

بِحُقُوقِ الْعَرَبِ . ٦- قَالُوا إِنَّ ذَلِكَ غَيْرُ مُمْكِنٍ الآنَ . ٧ -

أَتَنْتَكِرُ أَنَّ أَلْمَانِيَا لَمْ تَنْهَزِمْ فِي الْحَرْبِ الأَخِيرَةِ ؟ فَمَنِ

الْمُنْتَصِرُ؟ ٨- اِنْعَقَدَ اجْتِمَاعُ رُؤَسَاءِ الْوِزَارَاتِ وَحَضَرَهُ

عَدَدٌ مِنْ وُزَرَاءَ عَرَبٍ . ٩- اِضْطَرَبَتْ حَالَةُ الدُّنْيَا وَلَا نَعْرِفُ

الأَسْبَابَ . ١٠- لِمَاذَا لَا تَنْتَكِرُ فِي الأَمْرِ؟ لَعَلَّ الْحَقِيقَةَ

تَنْكَشِفُ لَكَ . ١١- اِنْقَلَبَتِ السَّيَّارَةُ فَانْكَسَرَتِ الْبَضَائِعُ .

١٢- إِذَا بِرَجُلٍ يَرْكَبُ حِصَانًا أَبْيَضَ . ١٣- قَسَمَ الشُّبَّانُ

كُلَّ شَيْءٍ . ١٤- أَمْثَالُ هَؤُلَاءِ الرِّجَالِ لَا يَعْتَرِفُونَ بِالْحَقِيقَةِ

حَتَّى لَوْ يَسْمَعُونَهَا . ١٥- اِنْصَرِفِي يَا بِنْتُ، وَاشْتَغِلِي

فِي الْمَطْبَخِ ، فَذَلِكَ وَاجِبُكِ . ١٦- أَمَرْتُكَ أَنْ تَقْتَرِبَ

مِنِّي، فَلِمَا لَا تَفْعَلُ ذلِكَ؟ ١٧- هُنَاكَ* اَضْطِرَابٌ
سِيَاسِيٌّ فِي الشَّوَارِعِ اليَوْمَ (فِي الشَّوَارِعِ اليَوْمَ اَضْطِرَابٌ
سِيَاسِيٌّ). ١٨- غَضِبْتُ مِنَ الكِسَارِ المُتَحَنِّينَ. ١٩-
تُفَكِّرُ جَدَّنِي أَنَّ شُبَّانَ اليَوْمِ كَسَالَى. ٢٠- لَا تَنْبَسِطُ
مِنْهُمْ.

Exercise 43

1. The king saw his daughter's blush(ing) when she met the foreign prince.   2. The horseman's face blanched (*or* went white) when the enemy approached him.   3. Do not blush, boy. I won't tell your father about what you did yesterday.   4. Use (a) pencil for your drawing.   5. We think it best that all the new members attend to hear the speech of the Russian and the American on these important matters.   6. Haste was the cause of that accident.   7. The company used many foreign workmen before the recent law.   8. America used the atom bomb against Japan in the war.   9. We shall not listen to your views (*or* opinions) in future.   10. The Japanese Prime Minister received (*or* welcomed) the ambassadors of the countries of Europe officially, and they spoke about Russia's policy.   11. They sat under the chairmanship of the Prime Minister of England.   12. Girls, draw pictures of this famous old Arab story.   13. "Hal" is an interrogative particle in Arabic.   14. We know nothing about that, so let

---

* "There is", "there are", are frequently translated in modern Arabic by هُنَاكَ placed at the beginning of the sentence. This word forms part of the predicate of a nominal sentence. The sentence above may literally be translated "a political disturbance (is) there in the street today".

us ask the professor (*or* teacher).   15. The Arab(ic) press is
very weak: as for the English press, we think highly of it.
16. They don't think much of (*or* think well of) the policy of
the nationalist party.   17. The rider hurried, so he fell off
his horse.   18. Bombs have been used in wars for a great
many years now (*lit.* since a great many years).   19. The sea
turned green, and the fear of the ship's passengers increased.
20. The White Nile is blue, so what is the reason for its
strange name?   21. I (really) have not heard that story.

Exercise 44

١- مَاذَا عَمِلْتِ يَا بِنْتُ؟ لِمَاذَا أَحْضَرْتِ؟ ٢- سَوْفَ
تَخْضَرُّ ٱلْجُنَيْنَةُ فِى ٱلصَّيْفِ بَعْدَ أَمْطَارِ ٱلرَّبِيعِ. ٣- لَا أَسْتَقِينُ
ٱلصِّحَافَةَ ٱلْإِنْكِلِيزِيَّةَ ٱلْيَوْمَ. ٤- نَنْتَظِرُ ٱلْإِصْلَاحَ فِى ٱلْمُسْتَقْبَلِ
فَذٰلِكَ سَبَبُ ٱلْقَانُونِ ٱلْجَدِيدِ. ٥- ٱلرَّأْىُ ٱلرَّسْمِىُّ (هُوَ) أَنَّ
ٱلْإِسْتِعْجَالَ ضَرُورِىٌّ لِهٰتَيْنِ ٱلدَّوْلَتَيْنِ لِأَنَّ ٱلْعَدُوَّ قَدِ ٱسْتَعْمَلَ
هٰذِهِ ٱلْأَسْلِحَةَ مُنْذُ سَنَوَاتٍ (سِنِينَ) كَثِيرَةٍ. ٦- ٱسْتَفْلَمْ
مِنَ ٱلْمُفَتِّشِ عَنِ ٱسْتِخْدَامِ ٱلْعُمَّالِ ٱلْيَابَانِيِّينَ فِى ٱلزِّرَاعَةِ.
٧- تَقَاتَلَتِ ٱلْعَدُوُّ (ٱلْأَعْدَاءُ) فِى أُورُبَّا. ٨- ٱسْتَقْبَلَ ٱلْمَلِكُ
أَعْضَاءَ ٱلْمَجْلِسِ فِى قَصْرِهِ. ٩- كَانَ ذٰلِكَ عَمَلَ ٱلْوَطَنِيِّينَ.
١٠- هُمْ تَحْتَ رِئَاسَةِ حَسَنِ عَبْدِ ٱللّٰهِ. ١١- إِنَّ قِصَّتَهُ

43

غَرِيبَةً جِدًّا. ١٢- كَانَ مُعَلِّمًا فِى جَامِعَةِ ٱلْقَاهِرَةِ.

١٣- اُسْتُخْدِمَ صَدِيقِى فِى سِفَارَةٍ أَجْنَبِيَّةٍ مُدَّةً طَوِيلَةً.

١٤- لٰكِنْ مَا ٱنْبَسَطَ هُنَاكَ، فَٱسْتَحْسَنَ أَنْ يَتْرُكَ
عَمَلَهُ. ١٥- وَقَعَتْ قُنْبُلَةٌ عَلَى سَيَّارَةِ ٱلْوَزِيرِ وَقَتَلَتْهُ.

١٦- اِسْتَعْمَلُوا (كَانُوا يَسْتَعْمِلُونَ) ٱلْقُوَّةَ ٱلذَّرِّيَّةَ. ١٧-
وَقَعَتْ قُنْبُلَتَانِ ذَرِّيَّتَانِ عَلَى ٱلْيَابَانِ فِى أَثْنَاءِ ٱلْحَرْبِ ٱلْأَخِيرَةِ.

١٨- لَا تَسْتَكْبِرِ ٱلصَّغِيرَ، لٰكِنْ لَا تَسْتَصْغِرِ ٱلْكَبِيرَ أَيْضًا.
تَذَكَّرْ قِصَّةَ دَاوُدَ. ١٩- رَسَمْتُ رَسْمًا لِهٰذِهِ ٱلصُّورَةِ،
لٰكِنَّ ٱلنَّاسَ ٱسْتَقْبَحُوهُ. ٢٠- مَا رَأْيُكَ فِى هٰذِهِ ٱلصُّوَرِ
ٱلْإِيطَالِيَّةِ، أَتَسْتَحْسِنُهَا أَمْ لَا؟

Exercise 45

1. The princess extended her hand to the Syrian prince, as
was her custom, and he kissed it. 2. The long road stretched
before us, so we prepared (ourselves) for the journey, and
felt joy in our hearts. 3. The women went mad when they
saw this scheme, but their menfolk (*or* men *or* husbands)
paid no attention to it (*or* were not bothered by it). 4. My
uncle was a thoughtful (*lit.* thinking) man who loved books
and study. 5. This book has been prescribed for all
Egyptian schools. 6. What is the story of that official?

Please tell me it.   7. The travellers prepared their horses for their journey to Syria.   8. (The) international companies must finish the scheme (*or* plan).   9. In any case, they have been compelled to co-operate with the government.   10. The chairman (*or* president, etc.) wrote concerning the question in one of the newspapers.   11. I was pleased that your deserts (*or* merits) were mentioned in the report.   12. The army of Syria joined the army of Egypt to help it in those difficult days.   13. The binding of the book was renewed. 14. Have you passed the people of the village near the well? 15. Collect the soldiers and count them at once.   16. This decision is very difficult in times of extreme cold.   17. My aunt thinks heat preferable to cold.   18. Hope makes men happy.   19. The wall of the house is very cold, whereas (*lit.* and) it was hot some hours ago.   20. Our joy was complete when the king ordered us to withdraw.

Exercise 46

١- قَدْ كَتَبَ ٱلْوَزِيرُ تَقَارِيرَ طَوِيلَةً عَنْ هٰذِهِ ٱلْمَسْأَلَةِ فَٱضْطُرَّتْ

ٱلْحُكُومَةُ (لِكَ) أَنْ تَفْعَلَ شَيْئًا لِلْمُوَظَّفِينَ لَلْمُسْتَحِقِّينَ . ٢-

تَطْلُبُ سُورِيَّا مَشْرُوعًا دُوَلِيًّا لِتَجَدُّدِ آمَالِ ٱلْأَهَالِى وَإِتْمَامِ

سَعَادَتِهِمْ . ٣- أُمِدُّ (رأُمِدِدُ) أَصْدِقَاءَكَ فِى أَوْقَاتِ ٱلضِّيقِ

كَعَادَةِ ٱلنَّصَارَى وَٱلْمُسْلِمِينَ وَٱلْيَهُودِ . ٤- اِعْتَرَفْتُ بِأَنَّهُ

قَدْ (رَكَانَ) جَنَّ مِنَ ٱلْحَرِّ . ٥- مَرَرْتُ بِمَبَانٍ كَثِيرَةٍ جَمِيلَــةٍ

* This translation assumes a connection with the previous one, هى
referring to شركات .

أَثْنَاءَ زِيَارَتِي لِلْغَرْبِ . ٦- قَدْ قَرَّتِ الْأُمُورُ فِى الشَّرِكَاتِ الْأَجْنَبِيَّةِ

٧- قَرَّرَتِ الْحُكُومَةُ أَنْ يَكُونَ النَّاسُ جَمِيعُهُمْ مُسْتَعِدِّينَ

لِيُقَاتِلُوا وَلِيَنْضَمُّوا إِلَى الْجَيْشِ فِى كُلِّ الْأَوْقَاتِ . ٨- قَصَّ

(اقْصُصْ) عَلَىَّ الْحِكَايَةَ (الْقِصَّةَ) لِأَنِّي أُحِبُّهَا كَثِيرًا . ٩-

يُحِبُّ الْإِنْكِلِيزُ سِبَاقَ الْخَيْلِ فِى فَصْلِ الْبَرْدِ (الْفَصْلِ الْبَارِدِ)

١٠- أَتَظُنُّهُ مَسْرُورًا ؟ ١١- يَغْضَبُ مِنْ قَرَارِ الْحُكُومَةِ . ١٢- لَا

أَهْتَمُّ بِالْمَسْأَلَةِ السُّورِيَّةِ . ١٣- الْأَمَلُ أَفْضَلُ مِنَ الْخَوْفِ .

١٤- تَمْتَدُّ الزِّرَاعَةُ مِنْ هُنَا إِلَى دِمَشْقَ .١٥- يَتِمُّ عَمَلِي بَعْدَ

أُسْبُوعٍ . ١٦- اذْهَبْ بِسُرْعَةٍ وَقُلْ لِذَلِكَ الرَّجُلِ الْمَارِّ أَنْ

يَنْتَظِرَ دَقِيقَةً . ١٧- فَلْتَسْتَحِقَّ (فَلْتَسْتَحْقِقْ) مَا عَمِلْتُ

لَكَ وَلِأَخِيكَ . ١٨- الْعَمَلُ لَا يَتِمُّ . ١٩- كُنْ مُسْتَعِدًّا

(اسْتَعِدَّ/اسْتَعْدِدْ) أَمَامَ الْبَابِ وَانْتَظِرْنِي .٢٠- إِنَّهُ مِنْ

وَاجِبِكَ أَنْ تَهْـــــــتَمَّ بِمُسْتَقْبَلِ وَطَنِكَ (بِلَادِكَ) .

Exercise 47

1. The Caliph was given the title of "Commander of the
Faithful" (*or* Prince of the Believers), on account of (*lit.* for)
his religious leadership.   2. The Muslim believes in God,

46

His angels, His prophets, His books, and the Day of Resurrection.   3. There are many religious words (*or* there is much religious vocabulary) in (the) Arabic dictionaries. 4. Our religion does not permit murder.   5. The guests asked permission to leave, and went off in a hired car, and the fare was two Egyptian piastres.   6. All (the) foreigners adopt this bad habit, and I hope that you will not adopt it, son.   7. The life of God's apostle has affected all Muslims. 8. You are a Muslim, so do not eat pork: that is forbidden in our religion.   9. Don't be late for my invitation.   10. I am certain that the traffic of cities harms humanity (*lit.* the human being).   11. It seems that the writing of books is not profitable these days.   12. All his wealth was dissipated (*lit.* went), so his father blamed (*lit.* blames) him.   13. Look at that blushing girl.   14. Certainty is not possible to authors of history books.   15. Show your politeness to the guests, son.   16. We are affected (*or* influenced) by the deeds (*or* works) of our ancestors.   17. Is there a car for hire in the street?   18. Their thoughts were like those of everybody. 19. The good teacher disciplines his (*lit.* the) pupils, but is not intimate with them.   20. The sun's heat is injurious (*or* harmful) in the East.

Exercise 48

١- أَكَلَ ٱلْخِنْزِيرُ فِي بَيْتِ ٱلنَّصْرَانِيِّ . ٢- كَيْفَ كَانَ ٱلْمُسْلِمُونَ يُلَقِّبُونَ خَلِيفَتَهُمْ؟ ٣- كَانُوا يُلَقِّبُونَهُ بِلَقَبِ » أَمِـيـن ٱلْمُؤْمِنِينَ « . ٤- أَمِنَتْ شُؤُونُ ٱلدَّوْلَةِ بَعْدَ قَتْلِ مُؤَلِّفِ ذَلِكَ ٱلْكِتَابِ ٱلْمُفَصَّلِ . ٥- ٱنْظُرْ تَأْثِيرَ ٱلْآرَاءِ ٱلدِّينِيَّةِ عَلَى رِقِّي) تَأْرِيخِ ٱلْعَالَمِ . ٦- ٱلدِّينُ شَيْءٌ مُهِمٌّ، أَهَمُّ مِنَ ٱلْمَالِ .

47

٧- أَقْبَلُ دَعْوَتَكَ ٱلْكَرِيمَةَ وَسَأُحَاوِلُ أَلَّا أَتَأَخَّرَ. ٨ -
لٰكِنِّي مَشْغُولٌ جِدًّا ، فَأَسْتَأْجِرُ سَيَّارَةً. ٩- تَسْتَحِقُّ
ٱلْأَفْكَارُ وَٱلْآدَابُ ٱلْعَرَبِيَّةُ دِرَاسَةً طَوِيلَةً. ١٠- آخَذَ مُحَمَّدٌ
ٱلنَّصَارَى وَٱلْيَهُودَ لِأَنَّهُمْ خَالَفُوا دِينَهُ. ١١- مَعَ ذٰلِكَ كَانُوا
يُؤْمِنُونَ بِيَوْمِ ٱلْقِيَامَةِ. ١٢- إِنَّ شُرْبَ ٱلْخَمْرِ مَمْنُـوعٌ
لِلْمُسْلِمِينَ. ١٣- لِهٰذَا ٱلْمُؤَلِّفِ تَأْلِيفَاتٌ (تَآلِيفُ/مُؤَلَّفَاتٌ)
كَثِيرَةٌ مَشْهُورَةٌ. ١٤- يَظْهَرُ أَنَّكَ قَدْ أَدَّبْتَ أَبْنَاءَكَ وَمَعَ
ذٰلِكَ يُؤَاخِذُونَكَ. ١٥- إِنَّ ٱلْمَلَائِكَةَ وَٱلرُّسُلَ عِبَادُ ٱللّٰهِ.
١٦- أَتَأَكَّدُ مِنْ أَنَّ هٰذِهِ ٱلْكَلِمَةَ مَوْجُودَةٌ فِى ٱلْقَامُوسِ. ١٧-
أُظْهِرُ فِرْشَيْكَ (غِرْشَيْكَ) لِصَاحِبِ ٱلْحِصَانِ ، لَعَلَّـهُ
يُؤَجِّرُهُ إِلَيْكَ. ١٨- فِى شَوَارِعِ بَغْدَادَ حَرَكَةٌ كَثِيرَةٌ. ١٩-
كَانَ ٱلْحَرُّ سَبَبَ مَرَضِهِ. ٢٠- لَا تَتَأَثَّرْ مِنْ آرَائِى ؛ فَكِّرْ
فِى ٱلْأَمْرِ.

Exercise 49

1. The Egyptian delegation was disgusted with recent events.
2. We ask God to help us in carrying out the plan. 3. Why do

you draw a good omen from the King's return when (*lit.* and) a government spokesman has announced that the problem has been solved? 4. Caesar's wife drew a good omen from his dream in the month of March. 5. I began reading the Qur'ān two months ago, and finished it within a whole month. 6. The executive authority put this law into effect as a means of reform. 7. The Iraq Petroleum Company informed the Iraq Government that the price of oil would be raised to two pounds a barrel in the new year. 8. The government (has) established light industries. 9. Follow the well-known plan, and fill your barrel with (the) olives. 10. I congratulate this company, because the relations of the management with the workers are very good. 11. We are in great need of independence, so let us pay its price. 12. The murderer escaped from prison, and took refuge in one of the village houses. 13. He found an axe there, but dared not use it. 14. He grew up in a small house near the city gate. 15. Begin the repair of the walls, workmen. 16. He manufactured swords for (the) brave men in one of his factories. 17. After some time (*lit.* the passage of time) the traveller returned to his homeland, and settled there. 18. Don't read this book, daughter. 19. Ask your teachers for the results of your examinations. 20. It is the people's duty to congratulate the Prime Minister on the success of the schema.

Exercise 50

١- هَنَّأَتِ ٱلْحُكُومَةُ ٱلْوَفْدَ عَلَى نَجَاحِهِ فِى سَبِيلِ تَحْسِينِ ٱلْعَلَاقَاتِ بَيْنَ ٱلشَّعْبِ وَٱلْإِدَارَةِ. ٢- صَرَّحَ مُتَكَلِّمٌ بِٱسْمِ ٱلْحُكُومَةِ بِرُجُوعِ ثَمَنِ ٱلنَّفْطِ لِمَا كَانَ (عَلَيْهِ) قَبْلَ ٱلْحَرْبِ. ٣- إِنَّ ٱلْحَيَاةَ سِجْنُنَا وَنَلْتَجِئُ إِلَى ٱلْأَحْلَامِ.

49

٤- قَدْ مَنَعَتْنَا الْحَوَادِثُ مِنَ الْحُرِّيَةِ مُنْذُ الْحَرْبِ وَنَحْنُ في

حَاجَةٍ إِلَيْهَا . ٥- أَصْبَحَ جِدَارُ هذِهِ الْحُجْرَةِ وَسِخًا

بِمُرُورِ الزَّمَانِ . ٦- اِبْتَدَأَ هذا النِّظَامُ التَّنْفِيذِيُّ قَبْلَ

أُسْبُوعٍ . ٧- وَصَلَنِي بِرْمِيلُ زَيْتُونٍ أَمْسِ . ٨- قَطَعَ الْخَدَمَةَ

(الخَادِمُونَ) الخَشَبَ بِنُؤُوسِهِمْ ، ثُمَّ تَبَأَّوا (نَبُّوا) أَصْحَابَهُمْ

بِإِتْمَامِ الْعَمَلِ . ١٠- قَدْ قَرَأْتُ جَمِيعَ الْقُرْآنِ (الْقُرْآنَ جَمِيعَهُ)

١١- أَتُفَأَّلُ بِإِنْشَاءِ هذِهِ الْمَصَانِعِ؟ ١٢- لا، أَشُاءَمُ عَلَيْهِ .

١٣- مَلَأْتُ فَنَاجِينَ الْضُّيُوفِ بِالْقَهْوَةِ فَشَرِبُوهَا. ١٤- نَشَأَ

هذا الْكَاتِبُ (الْمُؤَلِّفُ) في مَدِينَةِ بَغْدَادَ . ١٥- كَانَ مَرِيضًا

وَمَعَ ذلك بَدَأَ اِمْتِحَانَهُ . ١٦- النَّتِيجَةُ مَجْهُولَةٌ لِأَنَّهَا

في يَدِ اللهِ . ١٧- إِسْأَلِ (سَلِ) الْعُلَمَاءَ عَنْ ذلك الرَّجُلِ

الْعَظِيمِ ، فَإِنَّهُ سَئِمَ مِنْ حَيَاةِ الْمُدُنِ . ١٨- مَاذَا صَنَعَتِ

الْيَوْمَ؟ ١٩- لا تَسْأَلْنِي عَنْ ذلك - هُوَ سِرِّي . ٢٠- قَدِ

اِرْتَفَعَتْ أَسْعَارُ السُّوقِ في الْأَيَّامِ الْأَخِيرَةِ .

Exercise 51

1. Until help arrived (*lit.* the arrival of help) the soldiers despaired of the result of the fight, because their situation had become difficult. 2. We reached the car-park, and left our car in it. 3. The government gave the good news of the new Anglo-Egyptian Agreement. 4. The earth became dry, agriculture failed, and imports were greater than exports. 5. The prisoners must wake at once, and stand in their cells (*lit.* rooms) for the governor's inspection. 6. Don't put your hands on the table. 7. Ḥasan faced his enemy, with anger and despair in his heart. 8. An important letter came from him with the promise of help. 9. The author described the wonders of the world in a wonderful book. 10. Piety is one of the believer's qualities. 11. Cooks (*fem.*), do not make hard work of (what is) easy, but do your work in such a way that the difficult will become easy. 12. Do not move, prisoner, but (*lit.* and) describe to me your connection with these men. 13. You (*pl.*) must agree in these matters. 14. While he was lying on his bed it happened that an unknown man awakened him. 15. The women dried their clothes, put them on, and faced the soldiers. 16. What have you promised? Have you agreed with them? Then you have made me despair. 17. Move your hands. 18. We are in agreement with that in these days of difficulty. 19. Put your pens on your tables. 20. The camel went to water, and drank a lot, and did not stop till I arrived (*lit.* my arrival).

Exercise 52

١- السُّرْعَةُ لِلْغَضَبِ صِفَةٌ رَدِيئَةٌ. ٢- كَمْ تَنَاهَا وَعَدَتَّا مِنْ وَاجِبِكَ أَنْ تُقَدِّمَ أَكْثَرَ مِنْ ذلك. ٣- وَصَفْنَا كُلَّ هذه المَوَارِدِ كَيْ تَعْرِفَ أَنَّ التَّقْوَى أَفْضَلُ مِنَ الْيَأْسِ،

وَقَدْ وَضَعْنَا آرَاءَنَا فِى رَسَائِلِنَا الْكَثِيرَةِ إِلَيْكَ فِى أَثْنَاءِ مُدَّةِ

سَنَتَيْنِ . ٤ـ إِنَّ مَوْقِفَ أَحْبَابِنَا خَطِرٌ وَهُمْ يُوَاجِهُونَ صُعُوبَاتٍ

مِنْ كُلِّ جِهَةٍ . ٥ـ كَانَ يَيْئَسُ مِنَ الْحَيَاةِ قَبْلَ وُصُولِكَ .

٦ـ تُؤْنِسُنِى زَوْجَتِى لِأَنَّهَا تُوقِظُنِى كُلَّ يَوْمٍ صَبَاحًا (فِى

الصَّبَاحِ) . ٧ـ وَقَفْنَا فِى مَوْقِفِ الْعَرَبَاتِ (السَّيَّارَاتِ) فَنَزَلْنَا

مِنْ سَيَّارَاتِنَا . ٨ـ هَذَا الِاتِّفَاقُ بَيْنَ عَدُوَّيْنِ عَجِيبٌ

وَهُوَ مِنْ عَجَائِبِ الدُّنْيَا . ٩ـ الْكَلَامُ (الْقَوْلُ) يَسِيرٌ

لَكِنَّ الْأَعْمَالَ عَسِيرَةٌ . ١٠ـ قَدْ وَصَفَ صِفَاتِ الْعَرَبِ

بِدِقَّةٍ . ١١ـ يَيْبَسُ (جَفَّ، نَشِفَ) ذَلِكَ الْكِتَابُ الَّذِى

وَقَعَ فِى الْمَاءِ ، حَتَّى تَسْتَعْمِلَهُ مَرَّةً أُخْرَى لِدُرُوسِكَ .

١٢ـ اتَّجَهَ التِّلْمِيذُ لِمُعَلِّمِهِ وَيَبِسَ لِسَانُهُ مِنَ الْخَوْفِ . ١٣ـ

وَرَدَ الْحَيَوَانُ الْمَاءَ اتِّفَاقًا وَتَحَرَّكَ الشَّجَرُ (وَتَحَرَّكَتِ الْأَشْجَارُ)

١٤ـ حَاوَلْتُ وَصْفَ ذَلِكَ الْحَيَوَانِ لَكِنْ فَشِلْتُ لِسُرْعَتِهِ .

١٥ـ لِنَتَوَافَقْ (لِنَتَّفِقْ) وَنُيَسِّرِ الْأُمُورَ . ١٦ـ قَدْ عَسَّرَهَا

غَضَبُكَ . ١٧ـ سَوْفَ نَصِلُ بَعْدَ سَاعَتَيْنِ لِأَنَّ الطَّرِيقَ قَـدْ

52

عَسَر (قد أَمْسَى عَسِيراً) . ١٨- إِسْتَيْقِظْنَ يا نِسَاءُ
وَأَعْمَلْنَ وَاجِبَكُنَّ فِى المَطْبَخِ . ١٩- قد تَيَسَّرَ عَمَلى .
٢٠- لا أُرَافِقُكَ .

Exercise 53

1. The Arabs settled in some cities of Syria, but were not happy there. 2. We flew to a distant place in the desert, and stayed in the government rest-house. 3. The airport (*or* airfield/aerodrome) there was very small, but the aviator knew it of old (*lit.* from time). 4. We were in an English plane, and I slept in it during the flight (*lit.* journey) as was my custom at home. 5. But we were accompanied by two French tourists who had not previously visited the country. So they could not sleep. 6. Soil conservation has become one of the most important needs in the east. 7. Ḥusain was hit by a rifle bullet. The assailant is unknown, and the victim is my brother-in-law. 8. Do not shout when you flee, so that the enemy may know nothing of your movements. 9. I wished to visit the northern country, but I waited for spring to come, because of the severity of winter there, and the bitter cold (*lit.* increase of cold) in that season. 10. Honoured sir, I inform you that I can go to Damascus and return from there after two days' rest, as I told you. Your obedient servant, Ḥasan. 11. The weather is hot now, so let us rest for an hour here, so that we may restore our strength and preserve our health. 12. Why have you been (so) long in the market, wife? Maybe the merchants have sold you all their goods. 13. You have become weak through that work, but as for me, I am used to it. 14. Pass me a cup of fresh tea. 15. Your brother is afraid. Have you scared him? 16. No, he is easily scared. 17. May God prolong your

life. 18. The women's illness lasted long, but they died in
the end. 19. Keep away from me, you may be afflicted by
this dangerous disease. 20. Keep your secret, or (*lit.* and) at
any rate, don't speak about it to women and children.

Exercise 54

١- طَارَ مُفَتِّشٌ فى مَصْلَحَةِ صِيَانَةِ التُّرَابِ مِنَ المَدِينَـةِ
لِيَبْحَثَ فى المَسْأَلَةِ . ٢- رَجَعَ وَنَاوَلَ الوَزِيرَ تَقْرِيرَهُ. ٣-وَضَعَهُ
هذا عَلَى مَكْتَبِهِ، لكِنْ لَمْ يَسْتَطِعْ (مَا اسْتَطَاعَ) أَنْ يَفْعَلَ
شَيْئاً لِأَنَّ زَوْجَتَهُ جَعَلَتْ تَزُورُهُ كُلَّ يَوْمٍ بَعْدَ الظُّهْرِ فَتَرَكَ
أَكْثَرَ عَمَلِهِ لِكَاتِبٍ (مِنَ الكَتَبَةِ) .٤- نُرِيدُ أَنْ نَكْتُبَ عَنْ
هذا لِأَنَّ الصُّعُوبَاتِ قَدِ ازْدَادَتْ فى الحُكُومَةِ أَخِـــيراً .
٥- على كُلِّ مُوَظَّفٍ أَنْ يَعْمَلَ وَاجِبَهُ وَيُطِيعَ الأَوَامِرَ. ٦- كان
نَوْمُ الحَارِسِ سَبَبَ إِصَابَتِهِ بِرَصَاصَةٍ (مِنْ رصاصةٍ).٧-
صُورُوا بَنَادِقَكُم يا جُنُودُ ولا تَنِرُّوا أَمَامَ العَدُوِّ. ٨- كَمْ
مَرَّةً قُلْتُ ذلك لَكُم ، لكِنْ لَمْ تَسْتَمِعُوا ؟ ٩- يَجِبُ عَلَيْنَا
أَلّا نَقِيلَ فى أَوْقَاتِ الحَرْبِ . ١٠- وَصَلُوا بِطَائِرَةٍ وأَقَامُوا
فى مَكَانٍ قَرِيبٍ مِنَ المَطَارِ. ١١-كَانَتْ عَادَتُهُم أَنْ يَخْرُجُوا

54

كلَّ مَسَاءٍ وَيُخِيفُوا (يُخَوِّفُوا) السُّكَّانَ . ١٢- أَسْتَحْسِنُ
أَنْ تُسَافِرَ بِالجَوِّ كَالسَّيَّاحِ الآخَرِينَ (الأُخَرِ). ١٣- كَانَ حَسَنٌ
كَمَيَّارٍ شُجَاعًا وَمَاتَ فِي طَائِرَتِهِ . ١٤- خُذْ رَاحَتَكَ فِي الاِسْتِرَاحَةِ.
١٥- يَسُرُّنِي أَنَّ السُّلْطَاتِ قَدْ أَطَالَتْ إِقَامَتَكَ هُنَا .

١٦- اِسْتَرِحْ (خُذْ رَاحَتَكَ) وَأَعِدُ النَّظَرَ فِي هَذِهِ الأَوْرَاقِ .

١٧- لَعَلَّكَ تَجِدُ فِيهَا مَا لاَ يَسُرُّكَ . ١٨- قَدْ طَالَتْ زِيَارَتُكَ
فَأَسْتَحْسِنُ أَنْ تُيَسِّرَ حَالاً وَتَعُودَ إِلَى أَهْلِكَ وَأَقْرِبَائِكَ
وَوَطَنِكَ . ١٩- أَتَعْتَادُ آرَائِي أَمْ لاَ ؟ ٢٠- عَلاَقَاتُنَا مَعَ
حُكُومَتِهِ خَوَّفَتْ (أَخَافَتْ) أَعْدَاءَهُ كَثِيرًا .

Exercise 55

1. I beg you not to invite (*or* call) that man, because he
claims that he is the bravest soldier in the army of the
Caliph (*lit.* Commander of the Faithful). 2. Summon the
owner of the aircraft and ask him of what he is complaining.
3. Let us call the imprisoned merchant and tell him that we
have pardoned (*or* forgiven) him. 4. The group approached
and recited the Qur'ān in a loud voice (*or* loudly). 5. (So)
let there be hope in your words (*or* speech) instead of (the)
complaints. 6. The wife of the dead Caliph wept, then she
accepted their invitation. 7. Most of the infantry escaped
(with their lives) and were guided to a place in which there
were water and food. 8. We lunched in your house, so I

think it best that we dine at my house. 9. Give me bread
and butter so that I won't die. 10. I hope that the judge has
(*lit.* will have) met his uncle during his visit to Aden. 11.
The girl walked to visit her aunt, but she returned by bus.
12. Do not complain of what has passed: think of the future.
13. The judge built a new house in the Arab quarter, and
moved into it (*lit.* lived in it) last month. 14. 'Lead us in the
straight path.' 15. They remained standing a long time,
then two men among them fainted, and were overcome by
oblivion (*or* forgetfulness). (*Active of the Arabic changed to
passive in translation.*) 16. Servant, throw this letter in the
special air-mail box, in the hope that it (*lit.* perhaps it) will
reach my brother in England before Christmas. 17. Circumstances demanded (*or* required) that we educate our sons in
the Institute of Education. 18. God created us so that we
may return to him after death, and live in Heaven. 19. This
man is like a devil who is not pleased with righteous deeds.
20. Zaid remembered what had happened, but the rest of
the men forgot it. 21. The two of them (*or* they two) watered
their gardens with pure water. But they gave their cattle
bitter water to drink (*lit.* as for their cattle, they *etc.*). 22. I
found a dog in Gordon Street, so I took it (*lit.* carried it)
home, and called it 'Gordon' henceforward. 23. Let us meet
in the garden, as the weather is fine today. 24. The thieves
attended court, and were sentenced to imprisonment.

Exercise 56

١- كَانَ أَبُو بَكْرٍ، رَضِيَ اللّهُ عَنْهُ، أَوَّلَ خَلِيفَةٍ (الخَلِيفَةَ الأَوَّلَ)
فِى تَأْرِيخِ الدَّوْلَةِ الإِسْلامِيَّةِ. ٢- نَقْرَأُ فِى السُّورَةِ الفَاتِحَةِ
لِلْقُرْآنِ : اِهْدِنَا الصِّرَاطَ المُسْتَقِيمَ. ٣- رَكِبَ المُسَافِرُ

الأَجْنَبِيُّ جَلَّلَ سَرِيعًا ونَجَا ، فَشَرِبَ حَلِيبَ الجِمَالِ أَثْنَاءَ
شَهْرَيْنِ ووَجَدَهُ مُرًّا جِدًّا ، لِأَنَّهُ كانَ يَعْتَادُ حَلِيبَ البَقَرِ
٤- تَلاقَوْا فِى مَكَانٍ عالٍ ، وكانَ الجَوُّ صافِيًا هناكَ وقَـدْ
سَئِمُوا مِن دُخانِ المُدُنِ . ٥- سَوْفَ يَبْقَى حسنٌ هُنا
بَدَلًا مِن أَبِيهِ . أَمَّا سائِرُ الحاضِرِينَ فَلْيَتَنَزَّهُوا مَعَنـا ،
ثُمَّ نُعطِيهِم الهَدَايا فَيَسْتَطِيعُونَ أَن يَقُومُوا . ٦- كُنْتُ
أَلْقَاهُ كُلَّ يومٍ فِى البَامِ حِينَما كنتُ أُدَرِّسُ فِى مَعْهَـدِ
التَّرْبِيَةِ . ٧- نَأْمُلُ (نَرْجُو) أَن يُعامِلَ القاضِى هَؤُلاءِ
الرِّجالَ كَما يَسْتَحِقُّونَ حِينَ يَحْضُرُونَ أَمامَهُ . فَسَرَقُوا
مَكاتِيبَ كثيرةً مِن البَرِيدِ الجَوِّيِّ وفَتَحُوها ، ثُمَّ إذا لَم يَجِدُوا
دَراهِم فيها رَمَوْها فِى النَّهرِ . ٨- إنَّهم شَياطِينُ ويَخَافُهُـم
أَغْلَبِيَّةُ سُكَّانِ هذهِ المدينةِ . ٩- فِى الماضِى اشْتَكَى ناسٌ
كثيرونَ مِن أَعمالِ صدِيقِكَ ، لكِنْ عَفَوْنا عَنهُ ، والآنَ سَوْفَ
نَبْكِى ولكِنَّنا نُعاقِبُهُ أيضًا . ١٠- قالَ المُعَلِّمُ للبَناتِ : اجرِينَ
وللأَوْلادِ : امشُـوا . ١١- هل نَسِيتَ أَنَّ أَباكَ قد تُوُفِّىَ
57

الأُسْبوعَ الماضِيَ ؟ ١٢- خَلَقَنا اللهُ لَكِنْ نَذهَبُ إلى دارِ
البَقاءِ . ١٣- دَعوْتُكَ، فَأَذَنْ مِنّي وقُلْ لي عَن شَكوَاكَ .
١٤- ما كان القائدُ الأَجنَبِيُّ يَعلَمُ العَرَبِيَّةَ الصَحيحـةَ
فَسَمَّى المُنشَـاةَ "بالمَواشي" ! ١٥- أَنزِعُ الرَجُلَ الَّذي يَدَّعي
أَنَّ ابنَهُ نَبِيٌّ . ١٦- بَنَيتُما بيتاً جميلاً وسَقَيتُما بُستـانًا
جميلاً وَلَكِنَّكُما لَمْ تُرَبِّيا أَطفالَكُما : وهذا أَمٌ واجِباتِكُما
كوالِدَينِ ومُسلِمَينِ . ١٧- نَرجو أن (نَرجوكَ أن) تَتلُوَ
القُرآنَ في المَسْجِدِ غَدًا ، فَإنَّكَ خَيرُ تالٍ في القَرْيَةِ . ١٨ -
صَمَتَتْ قُلوبُنا . ١٩- دَعاني الوَزَراءُ لِأَتَعَشَّى مَعَهُمْ . ٢٠-
كانت هذه الدَعوَةُ غَيرَ مُتَوَقَّعَةٍ (مُنتَظَرَةٍ) ، ولا أَستَطيعُ أن
أَذهَبَ لِأَنّي مَشغولٌ تلك اللَيْلَةَ . ٢١- سَلَّمَ عَلَيها ومَضى
إلى بيتِ عَمِّهِ فَبَقِيَ هناك حتّى غُروبِ الشَمْسِ .

Exercise 57

1. A transmitter relates that the inhabitants of Merv gathered round their governor and shouted: 'Long live our noble (or generous) ruler.' 2. Can I attend this special case? 3. You did not benefit from your visit to the market since you sold

the eggs then lost the money. 4. A rich merchant married his pretty (*or* beautiful) daughter to an officer of the Iraq army. 5. Before this (*or* previously) that officer's driver, who was an army private, had wanted to marry her, but her father had refused. 6. Ḥasan was chosen as Assistant to the General Manager. 7. They saw a great city in the distance, so they walked towards its gate, entered it, and took refuge with its governor. 8. A sergeant was driving (*or* used to drive) the general's car. 9. How old are you? 10. A youth has been appointed minister, and we need a strong man. So what is the use of his appointment? 11. You have lived with us a year and done us no good. 12. The teacher called Zaid's name, and his friend replied: 'Absent'. 13. He was aflame with love of God, and thus he almost lived for religion. 14. When our sons came to us after a long absence, we were sad at their bad condition (*lit.* the badness of their condition).* 15. Tell us what you want. 16. I trod that foreign ground and found no-one to shelter me (*or* did not find any one who would shelter me). 17. My son returned from school and brought a nasty story. 18. You shall come in two days time, and see the reason for everything. 19. We did not see the like of this famous (person) in the Great World War.

Exercise 58

١- يُرْوَى أَنَّ القائِدَ قَادَ جَيْشَهُ فَ تَأَجُّجِ القِتَالِ وَرَجَعَ

مُنْهَزِماً ، فَأَوَى إِلَى سُكَّانِ مَرْوَ. ٢- لَا نَسْتَطِيعُ أَنْ نَحْضُنَ

هذه التَّفْضِيَّةَ فَ المَحْكَمَةِ لِأَنَّ المُصَابَ صَدِيقُنَا. ٣-

---

* In the *Grammar*, questions 15–19 have been erroneously numbered 16–20.

عَيَّنَ الضَّابِطُ نَفَرًا مِنَ الجَيشِ لِيَكُونَ سَائِقِي الخُصُوصِيَّ.

٤- قد أَحْيَا الرُّوَاةُ تَأْرِيخَ الإِسْلَامِ وَنَرَى المَاضِيَ فِى رِوَايَاتِهِمْ. ٥- يَحْيَى المَلِكُ. ٦- اِحْتَرَتُ جَارِيشًا (ثَارِبًا) لِأَنَّ الضُّبَّاطَ كُلَّهُم قدغَابوا. ٧- أَضَاعَ الخَادِمُ الطَّعَامَ فَاسْتَنْفَدْتُ مِن طَعَامٍ طَبَّاخِ جَارِهِ. ٨- عِشْتُ مُدَّةً طَوِيلَةً فِى البَادِيَةِ (الصَّحْرَاءِ) فلا أَحْتَاجُ إلى شَيءٍ. ٩- مَا وَطِئُوا أَرْضَ (تُرَابَ) وَطَنِهِمْ مُنذُ سَنَتَيْنِ، لَكِنَّهُـم سَيَرْجِعُونَ إِلَيْهِ بَعْدَ شَهْرٍ. ١٠- جِئْتُ، فَرَأَيْتُ، فَغَلَبْتُ.

١١- اِشْتَكَيْتُ مِن سُوءِ حَالِي، فَتَزَوَّجْتُ. ١٢- زَوَّجَنِى أَبِى بِامْرَأَةٍ قَبِيحَةٍ، كَانَ اسْمُها هِنْدًا. ١٣- آوَتْنِى لٰكِنْ مَا أَفَادَتْنِى (شَيئًا). ١٤- لَا تَسُقْ سَيَّارَتِى، فَأَنْتَ سَائِقٌ مَعِيبٌ. ١٥- آتِنِى تِلكَ البَيْضَ وَضَعْها على المَائِدَةِ. ١٦- قُلتُ لِلسَّائِلِ: مَاذَا تُرِيدُ مِنِّى؟ فَأَجَابَ: لَا أُرِيدُ شَيئًا مِن رَجُلٍ مِثْلِكَ. ١٧- فَوَائِدُ هذه الحُكُومَةِ الحَسَنَـةِ مَعْرُوفَةٌ عِندَ الجَمِيعِ. ١٨- اِذْهَبْ نَحْوَ المَدِينَةِ وَقِفْ عِندَ

الجسر. ١٩- آتِنِي لَحْمًا وَآتِنِي خَمْرًا . ٢٠- يُوجَدُ* جَبَلٌ
(تَلٌّ) فِي البُعْدِ ، وَيَرْوُونَ أَنَّ سَيِّدَنَا تُوُفِّيَ (مَاتَ) هُنَـاك
لِأَنْ (لِـ / كَيْ / لِكَيْ) يُنْقِذَنَا (يُخَلِّصَنَا) كُلَّنَا (جَمِيعًـا).

Exercise 59

1. They followed the Sufis' sect, so they wore woollen clothes. 2. We heard on Khartoum radio that a large number of elephants were seen in the Southern Sudan. 3. Consequently, the head of the central government veterinary surgeons travelled from the capital to see the animals' condition. 4. That man was a philosopher, and according to his philosophy (*lit.* in his philosophy that) the adornments of the world are among the evil suggestions of the Devil. 5. Engineers have special concessions in oriental countries. 6. I felt pain in the neck and throat, so I gargled. 7. This translator always stutters (in his speech) but his translation is very good. 8. He has translated the Qur'ān into Persian. 9. O proud man, your affairs will dwindle away in the future. 10. A boy rolled a stone from the roof of the house, and it fell on his uncle's head. 11. The boy shook the apple tree, and many apples fell from it. 12. The enemy army was repulsed, so our affairs will become tranquil. 13. When the governor pointed at us our hair stood on end and we trembled. 14. Khartoum is the administrative centre. 15. The local government has paid a large sum to reform the administration. 16. The dragoman showed me the famous sights of Cairo. 17. Adorn your hearts with piety, believers. 18. This man philosophises, but he knows nothing of philosophy.

*or . . . إِنَّ هُنَاك جَبَلاً

19. Speak clearly, and do not stammer. 20. The men pointed at (or referred to) the head of the administration.

NOTE: In sentence 20, the use of كان with the verb "to refer to, point at", would frequently imply the continuous or habitual past – "the men were referring to (pointing at)" or "the man used to refer to (point at)". In this, as in many other matters, the precise translation is determined by the context. But these exercises are mostly in single sentences, so the precise context is unknown, and several alternative translations are equally admissible.

Exercise 60

١- قد أُذِيعَ في العاصِمةِ أَنّ المَبْلَغَ المُحْتَاجَ إِلَيْهِ جُنَيْهانِ لِكُلّ سَاكِنٍ . ٢- أُشِيرَ إلى الأَمْرِ المَحَلّيّ عن تَعْيِينِ البَيَا طِرَةِ . ٣- هذا (هو) أَمْرٌ لِلْحُكُومةِ المَرْكَزِيّةِ .

٤- أَعْطَتِ الحُكُومةُ تُجّارَ الصّوفِ اِمْتِيَازَاتٍ خَاصّةً (رأَعْطَتِ الحُكُومةُ اِمْتِيَازَاتٍ خَاصّةً لِتُجّارِ الصّوفِ). ٥- لِمَاذَا تَتَمَذْهَبُ مَذْهَبَ النّصَارَى وأَنْتَ فَيْلَسُوفٌ ؟ ٦- الدّينُ أَفْضَلُ من الفَلْسَفَةِ فِيهِذِهِ سَوْفَ تَضْمَحِلُّ . ٧- اِقْشَعْرَرْنا لَمّا رَأَيْنا خَرَاطِيمَ الأَفْيَالِ . ٩- وَسْوَسَ الشَّيْطَانُ هذه الآرَاءَ في أُذُنَيْكَ . ١٠- تَزَلْزَلَتِ الأَرْضُ ، وتَدَحْرَجَتِ الصُّخُورُ

٨- اِهْدَأْ ولا تَشْغَلْ بالَكَ بِزَخَارِفِ الدُّنْيا

من الجِبَالِ وَتَنْتَمِ النَّاسُ فِى كَلَامِهِمْ . ١١- اِنْقَبَضَ حَلْقِى
وَكَانَ وَجَعٌ فِى عُنُقِى ، فَتَغَرْغَرْتُ بِمَاءٍ حَارٍّ (بِالمَاءِ الحَارِّ)
١٢- تَرْجَمْنَا هٰذَا الكِتَابَ كَىْ تَعْرِفُوا وَتُؤْمِنُوا . ١٣- كَانَ
يُبَيْطِرُ ، لٰكِنَّهُ الآنَ مُتَرْجِمٌ فِى مَكْتَبٍ مِنْ مَكَاتِـبِ
الحُكُومَةِ . ١٤- زُيِّنَتِ النِّسَاءُ وُجُوهَهُنَّ لِلْعِيـدِ .
١٥- أَصْبَحَ المُهَنْدِسُ مَشْهُورًا ، فَأَخْوَنْطَمَ . ١٦- دَخَـرَجَ
تِلْكَ المُدَخِّرَةَ الكَبِيرَةَ مِنَ البَابِ . ١٧- لِمَاذَا تَتَفَلَّتُ دَائِمًا
فِى أَوْقَاتِ الشِّـدَّةِ ؟ ١٨- هَاجَمُوا (هَجَمُوا على)* الحُدُودَ ،
لٰكِنْ (لٰكِنَّهُم) تَمَّهْثَرُوا وَانْهَزَمُوا . ١٩- مَا رَأْيُكَ (مَاتَفْكِرُ)
فِى الصُّوفِيَّةِ ؟ ٢٠- لَا أَعْرِفُ شَيْئًا عَنْهُمْ .

Exercise 61

1. That occurred during the two holidays (*or* two days of the
festival). 2. The people began to cry when the end of the
show (*or* exhibition) was announced. 3. The women began
to shout: "Down with colonisation! (*or* imperialism),'' and
they went on shouting until their voices weakened. 4. The
plane landed at the airport, the passengers disembarked
from it, and began to run to the manager's office. 5. I saw a

---

* After the form in brackets it would, of course, be الحُدُودِ

picture of my absent brother in the police gazette. 6. It is
the view of official circles that the economic state of our
region has scarcely improved since the beginning of the year,
and that is not propaganda. *7. Ḥasan went to the station, and
bought a ticket to Khartoum, then got on the train. 8. Perhaps Ḥasan will not return to us. 9. al-Bukhārī was (is) a
fine Ḥadīth recounter; he is the best writer of the Traditions.
May God have mercy on him! 10. How excellent and
beautiful is the Queen! We have not ceased to respect her
since her coronation day. 11. The merchants began to display
their wares for sale. 12. I entered his house, and he remained
seated, unable to rise, because he had not eaten anything for
(the period of) a week, nor had he (with him) any money
with which to buy food. 13. Who will fill (*or* fills) the place
of the founder of this school? 14. We attended a tea party
in the camp and met many soldiers there. 15. The minister
contacted newspaper proprietors, and that led to the improve-
ment of relations between the press and the government.
16. Seldom have the English rebelled during their long
history. 17. You have long been absent, and so have become
like a stranger or foreigner. 18. The club was opened on a
new basis, namely (*lit.* and it is), the payment of a pound per
year. 19. Muḥammad (may God bless him and save him!)
was God's prophet, and Abū Bakr (may God be pleased with
him!) his successor.

Exercise 62

١- ما أُحْسَنَ هذا المَعْرِضَ : فَيَسْتَفِيدُ النَّادِي مِنْهُ
كَثِيرًا . ٢- عِنْدَما حَضَرْتُ حَفْلَةَ دَائِرَةِ المُؤَلِّفِينَ
حَدَثَ لِي حَادِثٌ (شَيْءٌ) غَرِيبٌ . ٣- دَخَلَ عَسْكَرِيٌّ

الشُّرْطةِ يَبْحَثُ عن الثُّوَّارِ (الثَّائِرِينَ) .٤- كانَتْ تِلكَ المَحَطَّةُ تُذِيعُ دِعَايَةً كَبِيرَةً تَحْتَ اسْمِ "صَوْتِ الحُرِّيَّةِ". ٥- إنَّ عِلْمَ الحَدِيثِ مُهِمٌّ جِدًّا لِلْمُؤْمِنِينَ. ٦- ما كَادَتِ الحَرْبُ تَنْتَهِى فَابْتَدَأَتْ حَرْبٌ جَدِيدَةٌ، فَتَقَاتَلَتِ الدُّوَلُ الكُبْرَى* (الكَبِيرَةُ) مَرَّةً ثَانِيَةً .٧- أَسَاسُ السِّيَاسَةِ الاِقْتِصَادِيَّةِ الجَدِيدَةِ غَيْرُ سَالِمٍ (لَيْسَ سَالِمًا/بِسَالِمٍ) ٨- لا يَزَالُ حَسَنٌ يَحِلُّ مَحَلَّ مُدِيرِ المِنْطَقَةِ .٩- كانَ مُحَمَّدٌ (صَلَّى اللهُ عَلَيْهِ وسَلَّمَ) نَبِيًّا حَسَنًا. ١٠- كُلَّما قَرَأْتُ إِعْلانًا مِثْلَ ذلِكَ طُولَ حَيَاتِى .١١- اِتَّصَلَ أَبِى بِأَخِيهِ وَبَدَأَ سِيَاسَةَ اقْتِصَادٍ شَدِيدٍ. ١٢- قَالَ لِلتُّجَّارِ أَنْ يَعْرِضُوا بِضَائِعَهُمْ فِى المُعَسْكَرِ حَتَّى يَشْتَرِيَهَا العَسَاكِرُ (الجُنُودُ). ١٣- فَلْيَسْقُطِ الاِسْتِعْمَارُ، لِأَنَّهُ لَيْسَ أَسَاسًا لِحُكُومَةٍ سَالِمَةٍ. ١٤- تُعْلَنُ أَوْقَاتُ القِطَارَاتِ فِى الجَرَائِدِ اليَوْمِيَّةِ. ١٠- ما دَامَتِ التَّذَاكِرُ غَالِيَةً سَأُسَافِرُ بِالحِمَارِ.

١٦- جَعَلَ يَضْعُفُ بَعْدَ تَتْوِيجِهِ ؛ رَحِمَهُ اللَّهُ! إِنَّهُ فِى

مَكَانٍ أَفْضَلَ الْآنَ . ١٧- وَقَعَتْ حَجَرَتَانِ مِنَ الْحَائِطِ

لَكِنَّى لَمْ أَهْتَمَّ (أُفَكِّنْ) بِهِما . ثُمَّ بَعْدَ شَهْرٍ انْكَسَرَ

الْحَائِطُ كُلُّهُ وَوَقَعَ . ١٨- أَصْبَحَ التَّاجُ مُهِمًّا. ١٩- قَرَأَ الْقُرْآنَ

كُلَّهُ ، ثُمَّ عَادَ (عادَ يَقْرَأُهُ). ٢٠- ذلك مِنْ وَاجِبَاتِ كُلِّ مُسْلِمٍ،

(وَاجِبُ كُلِّ ... / وَاجِبٌ على كُلِّ ...)

Exercise 63

I had formed the desire to penetrate into the Land of Dark-
ness, and it is entered from Bulghār.* Between the two is a
journey of 40 days. Then I gave that (idea) up, because of
the great (*lit.* greatness of the) trouble and lack of provisions
there. One can travel there only by small sledges drawn by
big dogs, for in that wilderness there is ice; (*the definite
article is not to be translated here*) and neither foot of man nor
hoof of beast grips in it. But (*lit.* and) dogs have claws, so
their feet grip in the ice. This country can only be entered
by powerful merchants who have each a hundred or so
sledges, loaded with their food, drink and wood. For there
are no trees in that country (*lit.* it), no stones and no settle-
ments. In that territory the guide is the dog who has travelled
in it frequently, and its value is as high as a thousand dinars
or thereabouts. The sledge is harnessed (*lit.* tied) to its neck,
and three dogs are yoked with it, and it is the leader. The rest
of the dogs follow it with (other) sledges, and whenever it
stops, they stop.

* Usually translated as the land of the Bulgars.

Exercise 64

١ـ دَخَلْتُ البَيْتَ وخِفْتُ من الظُّلْمَةِ فيهِ . ٢ـ لَنُدْتُ على مَسَافَةِ أَرْبَعِينَ مِيلًا من بَيْتِى ؛ لِذلِك أَذْهَبُ هناك لِأَشْتَرِىَ أَغْلَبِيَّةَ (أَكْثَرَ) اِحْتِيَاجَاتِى (حاجَاتِى) .

٣ـ لِلْعَرَبَةِ أَرْبَعُ عَجَلاتٍ . ٤ـ لا تَجُرُّرْ هذه الأشْيَاءَ فى الجَلِيدِ . ٥ـ خِفْتُ (كنتُ أُخَافُ) مِن قِلَّةِ الجَدْوَى فى المَفَازَةِ . ٦ـ نَحْتَاجُ لِلى حَطَبٍ لِلنَّارِ لِأَنَّ الشِّتَاءَ قَدِ ابْتَدَأَ . ٧ـ الحِمَارُ دَابَّةٌ مُفِيدَةٌ . ٨ـ أَوْقِرْجَمَلَيْنِ بِماءٍ . ٩ـ كان حسَنٌ أَحَدَ أَدِلَّائِنَا . ١٠ـ تَثْبُتُ أَظْفَارُ لِلْحَيَوَانَاتِ الوَحْشَةِ فى الأَرْضِ . ١١ـ أَصْبَحَ ثَمَنُ اللَّحْمِ غالِيًا مُنْذُ الحَرْبِ . ١٢ـ أُرْبِطْ حِصانَكَ لِتِلْكَ الشَّجَرَةِ . ١٣ـ لِهذا الحَيَوَانِ قَرْنَانِ طَوِيلَانِ . ١٤ـ هذا هُوَ قَرْنُ التَّقَدُّمِ . ١٥ـ لَنَا ثِيرَانٌ كثيرةٌ لكِنَّا (لكِنَّنا) نَحْتَاجُ إلى زِيَادَةٍ بَقَرَاتٍ (بقرات أَكْثَرَ) . ١٦ـ تَثْبُتُ حَوافِرُ لِلجِمَالِ فى الصَّحْرَاءِ (البَادِيَةِ/المَفَازَةِ) . ١٧ـ فى الشِّتَـاءِ

67

الإنكليزيّةِ الشَّـديدِ . (هناك) جَليدٌ (ثَلْجٌ) كثيرٌ، خُصوصاً

فى الشَّـمالِ . ١٨ - ما قيمَـتُهُ هذا الذَّهَبِ ؟ ١٩- قيمَتُـهُ

جُنَيهانِ . ٢٠ - أنْتُم قليلُونَ ، وَنَحْنُ مِـائةٌ .

Exercise 65

1. Listen to words (*lit.* speech) which come from the heart.
2. The answer to this question is "No" as I told you before.
3. The men decided on that course as if (the) devils had
settled in their hearts. 4. I did not see the singers who sang
that song. 5. The battle in which the Arabs and Christians
fought each other was one of the most important battles in
the Middle Ages. 6. We are the two travellers who travelled
in the Mediterranean and Red Seas and the Persian Gulf.
7. This is a high mountain, higher than the one (*lit.* mountain) which was described in your statement. 8. The peoples
of Africa desire independence and self-government. 9. Take the
necessary steps. 10. The robber who fired on us the day before
yesterday had with him a quantity of pearls. 11. The Caliph
said in his sermon : "Do not adorn your bodies with those things
which the poor do not enjoy." 12. Our family armed themselves, and their blood flowed in that war. 13. In my garden
are roses (*lit.* rose flowers) which arouse our emotions.
14. Our desire for that is known to you all. 15. We do not
doubt that the speech of His Majesty the King is a glorious
speech which deserves mention. 16. The problems of the
foreign minister go back to the days of the Ottoman Empire.
17. We had great doubt as regards (*lit.* in the matter of) the
emperor, although his glory had influenced the history of the
East and the West. 18. He is a glorious king whose name
will not be forgotten in the future. 19. The two girls who
arrived from Baghdad have lost their (two) trunks in the
train. 20. Do not listen to (the) foreigners' propaganda.

Exercise 66

١- الغُرَابُ الَّذِى أَرْسَلْتَهُ أَمْسِ لا يَطْلُبُ أَىَّ تَشْكِينٍ. ٢-
كَانَتِ الخُطْبَةُ الَّتِى سَمِعْنَاهَا فى الجَامِعِ مَجِيدَةٌ ، لكنَّها ما ذَكَرَتِ
الدَّمَ الَّذِى سَالَ فى مَعَارِكِ العَرَبِ. ٣-عَزَمَ على أن يُطْلِقَ
النَّارَ على عَائِلَتِى لكنّه لَمْ يُوَفَّقْ. ٤- كان لِحَسَنٍ كَمِّيَّةُ
لآلِئَ (كمِيَّةٌ مِن اللَّآلِئ) قَدْ أُرْسِلَتْ إليْهِ مِن إفْرِيقِيَا. ٥-
كَمَا قُلْتَ أَوَّلَ أَمْسِ ، كانَتْ أُغْنِيَّةُ هذا المُغَنِّى (هذه المُغَنِّيَةِ)
تُشِيرُ إلى الحُكْمِ الذَّاتِى. ٦- لا تَسْتَمِعْ لِلَّذِينَ (و لِ + الَّذِينَ)
يُزَيِّنُونَ بُيُوتَهُمْ بِالزُّهُورِ. ٧- نَتَمَتَّعُ بِالفَوَائِدِ الَّتِى ذَكَرَها
وزِيرُ الخَارِجِيَّةِ، مع أنَّنا نَشُكُّ فى حَلِّ المُشْكِلَةِ. ٨- قـد
أُثِيرَتْ عَوَاطِفُنَا، لكنْ شُكُوكَنَا ازْدادَتْ مُنْذُ قِيَامِ جَلالَةِ
المَلِكِ لِيَزُورَ الإمْبَرَاطُورَ. ٩- قدِ انْتَهَتْ إمْبَرَاطُورِيَّتُـهُمْ
لكنْ مَجْدَها يَبْقَى. ١٠- يَبْقَى شَكُّنا كَأَنَّا لا نَزَالُ فى
أوْقاتِ الظُّلْمَةِ. ١١- اتَّخَذْنَا التَّدَابِيرَ اللَّازِمَةَ لإلْغَـاءِ
القَانُونِ الجَدِيدِ. ١٢- جَبَلُ صِنِّينَ أَعْلَى مِن الجِبَالِ الَّتِى

69

زُرْتَهَا : إِنَّهُ أَعْلَى جَبَلٍ فِى لُبْنَانَ . ١٣ - أُذِيعَ بَيَانٌ آخَرُ .
١٤ - قَدْ عَبَرْنَا البَحْرَ الأَبْيَضَ المُتَوَسِّطَ مَرَّتَيْنِ . ١٥ -
العَسْكَرِيُّ الَّذِى ذَكَرْنَا اسْمَهُ عَبَرَ الخَلِيجَ الفَارِسِيَّ وَزَارَ
بِلَادَ العَرَبِ . ١٦ - البَحْرُ الأَحْمَرُ مَشْهُورٌ فِى تَأْرِيخِ اليَهُودِ .
١٧ - هُوَ البَحْرُ الَّذِى عَبَرُوهُ حِينَمَا قَامُوا مِنْ مِصْرَ وَقَصَدُوا
فِلَسْطِينَ . ١٨ - هُوَ جَبَلٌ عَالٍ . ١٩ - تَسَلَّحَ المِصْرِيُّونَ .
٢٠ - إِنَّ مَحَبَّتَنَا لِلِاسْتِقْلَالِ هِىَ الَّتِى أَدَّتْ إِلَى قِيَامِنَا
(أَنْصَارِنَا) مِنْ مِصْرَ وَسَفَرِنَا إِلَى فِلَسْطِينَ ، لِأَنَّ الحُكْمَ
الذَّاتِيَّ خَيْرٌ مِنَ الحُكْمِ الصَّالِحِ .

Exercise 67

1. If (only) the fire brigade had arrived two hours ago, the
fire would not have spread to the neighbouring buildings.
2. If you had said the afternoon prayer, we would have been
able to leave at once. 3. Were it not for this merchant the
fire would have been put out. 4. If the wounded die, you
are responsible, doctor. 5. When (if) the wife puts meat on
the table, the dog eats it; for this reason she would always
put it in the cupboard. 6. He was the leader, and when (if)
he halted, the rest halted, as is customary in the organisation
of caravans. 7. If he betrayed his king, then he was the
worst traitor in the history of our country; and if he did not
betray him, historians have lied. 8. If he worships idols he is

70

an unbeliever. 9. If the minister demands proof, show him this letter in which there is the name of your companion, and say to him: "Here is the name of him who accompanied me in my long journey, so consult him if you wish." 10. When (if) an eloquent preacher preaches to them they do not listen to his sermon. 11. If you undertake this work through a contractor, you will succeed in due course (*or* later); and if not, you will see your endeavour is in vain. 12. If I bury my son, I bury my hopes with him. 13. If I give you the sun and the moon, you will certainly not be contented with them! 14. If those two found a boat they crossed the river, they and their party. 15. If you do not sow you will have no harvest to reap. 16. Whenever the soldiers found their foes they killed them. 17. Whatever evil happens, live contented. 18. He who forgets the ties of friendship is not a friend. 19. Please your mother and you will please your father because he loves her. 20. You will extinguish the fire of our friendship if you pour upon it the water of doubt.

Exercise 68

١- إِنْ (رِإِذَا) أَنْدَفَقَ (إِنْ/إِذَا يَنْدَفِقْ) مَاءٌ سُخْنٌ
فى الدَّوَالِيبِ ، فَسَيَكُونُ جَمِيعُ عَمَلِ المُتَعَهِّدِ بَاطِلاً.
٢- لَوْلاَ هذا الوَاعِظُ الرَّدِىءُ البَلِيغُ كانَ سُكَّانُ القَرْيَةِ
قَدِ اقْتَنَعُوا بِما عِنْدَهُم. ٣- لَوْ أَنَّكَ قد سَـاعَدْتَ
(رِسَاعَدْتَ) الجَرْحَى ، لَمَا وَقَعُوا فى أَيْدِى ذلك العَدُوِّ

* The alternative use of إِنْ and إِذَا in *Conditional Sentences* will not usually be shown in the Key – nor will the alternative use of the *Perfect* and *Jussive*.

71

الخَائِن . ٤- لَوْ شَاهَدتَّ ما حَدَثَ لِلْكُفَّارِ الَّذِينَ عَبَدُوا
(يَعْبُدُونَ) الأَصْنَامَ ، لَدَفَنْتَ شُكُوكَكَ ، وأَقْنَعَتْكَ
كَلِمَاتُ النَّبِي . ٥- إِنْ (إذا) تُصَلِّ (صَلَّيْتَ) صَلاةَ
العَصْرِ حالاً ، نَسْتَطِعْ (نَقْدِرْ) أَنْ نَقُومَ مع قافِلَةِ
مَكَّةَ . ٦- إذا نَفْتَحِ الشُّبَّاكَ تَدْخُلِ الرِّيحُ فى الحُجْرَةِ
وإذا نَفْتَحِ البابَ يَدْخُلِ المَطَرُ . ٧- لَوْ طَلَبَتْ بِنْتِى
بُرْهانًا ، قُلْتُ لَها ما وُعِظَ فى الخُطْبَةِ فى المَسْجِدِ أَمْسِ.
٨- إِنْ لَمْ يُرْضِهِ ما كان على الطَّاوِلَةِ (المائِدَةِ) أَخَذَ
ما فى الدَّوالِيبِ أَيْضًا . ٩- إِنْ عَمِلَ بِوَاسِطَةِ هـذا
الفَرِيقِ ، فالنَّتِيجَةُ فى أَيْدِيهِم ، لأَنَّهُ لَيْسَتْ لَهُ سُلْطَةٌ
عَلَيْهِم . ١٠- إِنْ تَرَ حَرِيقًا فَنادِ * فِرْقَةَ المَطافِئِ
فإِنَّها تَجِىءُ بِسُـرْعَةٍ ونُطْفِئُهُ .١١- إذا كان لَهُ رَفِيقٌ
ما خَافَ مِنَ الأَخْطارِ . ١٢- إِنْ لَمْ تَجْتَهِدْ فإِنَّكَ لاتَنْجَحُ.
١٣- مَهْمَا كان الحالُ ، إِنَّ المَحاصِيلَ رَدِيئَةٌ هذه السَّنَةَ

---

* *Imperative of* نَادَى (ندو) III) with) نَّ.

72

والسَّبَبُ عَدَمُ (قِلَّةُ) المَاءِ . ١٤- إِن غِبتَ مِن البَيتِ
مُدَّةً طويلةً ، أَنطَفأَتِ النيرانُ . ١٥- ما تَزرَعْ تَحصِدْ .
١٦- إِن لَم تَجِدْ مَركَبًا فى النَّهرِ، فَلَيسَ ذلك مِن غَلطِى .
١٧- مَن خان وَلَكِنهُ اَستَحَقَّ المَوتَ . ١٨- أَينَما ذَهَبتَ
رافَقتُكَ . ١٩- كُلَّما أَراك (رأَيتُكَ) تَذَكَّرتُ أُمِّى . ٢٠- عِشْ
قَنِعًا فى المُستَقبَلِ ، تَجِدْ (وَجَدتَّ) رَوابِطَ الصَّداقَـةِ
مُساعَدةً كبيرةً ، وسَوفَ تَحصُلُ على ما هو أَنفَسُ
مِن المالِ - وهو بالٌ مُطمَئِنٌّ .

Exercise 69

1. A government spokesman declared yesterday that one of
the ministers had resigned, and what increases the Prime
Minister's difficulty is (the fact) that the reason for the resignation is unknown. 2. The new mistress entered the class to
teach the girls history, but she only found one of them, and
she was a refugee. 3. Give me two nails only, and put the
rest of the nails in that big box. 4. Three shepherds went out,
with (*lit.* and with them) 9 sheep, 25 camel mares, and two
(male) camels. 5. Have you visited the zoological garden in
Beirut? There are four young elephants and many camels.
6. The Seven Mu'allaqāt are among the most famous odes
in Arabic poetry. 7. In our village there is one doctor now:
there were two before the war. 8. Eight women approached
the city gate after the Germans' attack, and they were

carrying their children. 9. Cow's milk is better than goat's milk, especially if it remains cold in the refrigerator. I have told you that a thousand times. Then why do you buy goat's milk and leave it in the sun? Come to your senses, servant! 10. We learn much of the thoughts of the subjects of the Caliphs of Baghdad from the book "A Thousand and One Nights", but these stories are unsuitable for the young in some places. 11. When I was crossing the Sahara (*lit.* the greatest desert) in 1925, I met six old <u>sh</u>aikhs who had never seen a foreigner before that day, so they attacked me. 12. Then I showed them my permit from the governor, but that increased their doubts of me (*lit.* of my affair) and their fear of me. 13. The Lebanon imported 1000 or so refrigerators last year, and she will import more than that quantity (*or* amount) in the coming year. 14. And she exported much fruit from the port of Beirut in that period. 15. Nineteen centuries have passed since the birth of Christ. 16. Ḥasan used to wake up in the morning and drive his father's sheep to a place far from home, and he had no watch. So in the evening he would ask every passer-by: "What time is it, sir?" 17. This country has been a republic for (*lit.* since) three years, and the government's policy pleases everybody (*lit.* the public). 18. I was born in London in 1914 A.D. 19. The visitor hung his dirty clothes on the big tree on Sunday, and left on Wednesday. Today is Saturday and his clothes are still hanging on the tree. 20. I spoke to the majority of the inhabitants of the village, with regard to (*or* on the occasion of) the loss of the <u>sh</u>aikh's sheep.

Exercise 70

١- فَتَحَتْ أُخْتِي أَحَدَ الصُّنْدُوقَيْنِ* فَقَطْ، فَفِي الآخَـرِ

مَسَامِيرُ طَوِيلَةٌ كَثِيرَةٌ، وَلَمْ تَفْتَحْهُ مُنْذُ جَاءَتْ مِن

* *lit.* one of the two boxes.

فِلَسْطِينَ مع اللَّاجِئِينَ . ٢- لِمَاذَا عِنْدَكَ تِلْكَ (ثَلَاثُ)
ثَلَّاجَاتٍ (بَرَّادَاتٍ) فى بَيْتِكَ ، وتَقُولُ إِنَّكَ رَاعٍ فَقِيرٌ؟
٣- جَاءَ وَاحِدٌ ، وغَابَ وَاحِدٌ ، لِأَنَّهُ (كَانَ) يَرْغَبُ فى
أن يَزُورَ حَدِيقَةَ الحَيَوَانَاتِ . كانَ أَثْنَانِ هذه السَّنَةَ .
ودُعُوتُ ثَلَاثَةُ السَّنَةَ المَاضِيَةَ ، لَكِنْ تُوُفِّيَ (مَاتَ) واحِدٌ
(أَحَدٌ) فى فِبْرَايَرَ (شُبَاطَ) ، رَحِمَهُ اللَّهُ . ٤- أَنَا رَجُلٌ
مُسِنٌّ الآنَ ، لَكِنِّى لا أَسْتَطِيعُ أن أَقُولَ إِنَّ سَعَادَتى
قَدِ ازْدَادَتْ مُنْذُ شَبَابِى . لِى ثَمَانِيَةُ بَنِينَ وثَلاثُ بَنَاتٍ
لَكِنْ تَزَوَّجَ كُلُّهُمْ وتَرَكُوا البَيْتَ. ٥- صَرَّحَ الوَزِيرُ فى
بَيَانِهِ بِمُنَاسَبَةِ حَالِ الجُمْهُورِيَّةِ الاِقْتِصَادِيِّ ، أَنَّ الوَارِدَاتِ
أَكْثَرُ مِن الصَّادِرَاتِ . ٦- قَدْ صَدَّرَتِ البِلَادُ سَبْعَةَ عَشَرَ
أَلْفَ سَيَّارَةٍ فى السَّنَةِ المَاضِيَةِ ، لَكِنَّها قَدِ اسْتَوْرَدَتْ
بَضَائِعَ قِيمَتُها أَكْثَرُ مِن ذلك . ٧- يَتَعَلَّقُ مُسْتَقْبَلُ البِلَادِ
بِالتِّجَارَةِ ، وهُناك مِائَةُ سَبَبٍ لِلصُّعُوبَاتِ (لِلْمَشَاكِلِ)
الحَالِيَّةِ (الحَاضِرَةِ) . وقَالَ : مع ذلك ، أَنَا المَسْؤُولُ فَأَسْتَقِيلُ

٧٥

٨- نَقْرَأُ فى تأْرِيخِ العَرَبِ أَنَّ القَصَائِدَ السَّبْعَ المَعْرُوفَةَ بِالمَعَلَّقَاتِ عُلِّقَتْ (تَعَلَّقَتْ) بِمَكَّةَ . وَيَقُولُ بَعْضُ العُلَمَاءِ إِنَّها عَشْـر ٠ ٩- هو فِلَسْطِينِيٌّ، لكِن دَرَسَ فى أَلْمَانِيَا وَأَصْبَحَ دُكْتُورًا سَنَةَ أَلْفٍ وتِسْعِ مِائَةٍ وخَمْسٍ وثَلاثِينَ .

١٠- يَكُونُ لِبِلادِنا مِيناءً جديدٌ فى السَنَةِ الآتِيَةِ يَصْلُحُ لِأَكْبَرِ سُفُنٍ ٠ ١١- لِسَبْتَمْبَرَ (لِأَيْلُولَ) ثَلاثُونَ يومًا ولأُكْتُوبَرَ (لِتِشْـرِينَ الأَوَّلِ) وَاحِدٌ وثَلاثُونَ، ولِفِبْرَايِـرَ (لِشُبَاطٍ) ثَمَانِيَةٌ وعِشْرُونَ أَو تِسْعَةٌ وعِشْرُونَ، فَقَط . ١٢- اِشْتَغَلْتُ مع الغَنَمِ والمَعْزِ أُسْبُوعًا، ثُـمَّ اِسْتَغَلْتُ ؛ والآنَ أَشْتَغِلُ مع الإِبِلِ، والحَقِيقَةُ أَنِّى أُرِيدُ أَن أَشْتَغِلَ مع الأَفْيَالِ . ١٣- هَجَمَتْ هذه القَبِيلَةُ على قَافِلَةٍ قَبْلَ أَيَّامٍ (قَلِيلَةٍ) وقَتَلَتْ نَحْوَ مِائَةِ رَجُلٍ وزَيَّدَ هذا الهُجُومُ خَوْفَ الجُمْهُورِ لِلعَرَبِ . ١٤- لا أَعْرِفُ كَم السَّاعَةُ فَلَيْسَتْ مَعِى سَاعَةٌ . ١٥- فَقَدْتُها يومَ الأَحَدِ فى اللَّيْلِ عِنْدَما (حِينَما) كنتُ أَذهَبُ من بيتِى

76

إلى بيتِ صَدِيقِي. ١٦- فَتَّشتُ عَنها يومَ الاثنَينِ صَباحًا.

١٧- وُلِدَ هذانِ الوَلَدَانِ في سنةِ ١٩٣١ م. ١٨- قابَلْتُهُ في

شَهرِ رَمَضانَ سنةَ ١٣٧٠ هـ. ١٩- عُمرُ ابْنَتِكَ الكُبرَى

كَمْ (سنةً)؟ عُمرُها سَبعَ عَشرةَ سنةً وعُمرُ ابنِي الأَصغَرِ

ثَلاثُ سِنينَ. ٢٠- قَضَيتُ العيدَ في بُستانِي (جُنَينَتي).

هُناكَ فيهِ (فيها) اثنَا عَشرَةَ شَجَرَةً مِنَ التُّفّاحِ لكنّ

أبناءَ جارِي أَخَذُوا كثيرًا مِنَ الفَواكِهِ. ٢١- سَمِعتُ

أنّكَ لَكَ خَمسونَ بَقَرًا وتِينَكٌ. فَلِماذا تَشتَري لبَنًا

(حَليبًا) مِنَ السُّوقِ؟

Exercise 71

1. The former chairman of the Nationalist Party says that
the researches of scholars have confirmed that this year is
the 87th (year) in the history of the party, and it is the oldest
party in our country: it is much older than the Socialist
Party – that is to say the Labour Party – and the Communist
Party. 2. This month is called "Dhū l-Qaʿda", and it is the
eleventh month. 3. We beg you to honour us by your
presence at our house on the 1st January. 4. The party will
be held in my house, which was formerly the house of the
vice-consul in Morocco. 5. I bought it from him when he
resigned, following the start of the crisis, and went (*lit.*
travelled) to the Maghrib. 6. We entrust ourselves to God

77

who gave success to the early (*lit.* first) Muslims in the early 7th Century. He will surely give the Muslims success in the future, because success is from God, not from anyone else. 7. The word "majlis" is used to mean "parliament" in some Eastern countries. 8. A long discussion took place in the Security Council of the United Nations about the problems of the continent of Africa, and the representatives of Asia presented a new programme to solve these problems as quickly as possible. 9. He asked the nation to fight as it had fought in the past. 10. We learned this from the correspondents of the major western newspapers. 11. In this book there are contents of great benefit to the Sunnites and also the Shi'ites. 12. You have honoured me by your visit, so I beg you to come again one day. 13. The king's palace consists of several parts: about one-fifth of it is a private residence for the king and his relations, another fifth is servants' quarters, and the remaining three-fifths are used as offices for the ministers and members of the government. 14. The nobles were three per cent of the subjects, but they nevertheless owned half the land(s). 15. In Arabic bi-literal, tri-literal and quadri-literal verbs are (to be) found. 16. The fort was built in the form of a large square. 17. The prisoners went out two by two. 18. Why have you drawn a triangle when I said to you: "Draw a hexagon (*or* six-sided figure)?" 19. I was in Algeria (*or* Algiers) last year, and met my cousin six times. 20. I visited Beirut for the third time in the middle of September.

Exercise 72

١- أَسَّسَ أُوَّلَ جَرِيدَةٍ وَطَنِيَّةٍ ظَهَرَتْ فِى العَالَمِ الشَّرْقِىِّ
وَتَمَاثِيلُ "التَّايِمِس" فِى بِرِيطَانِيَا ٢٠- أَطْلَقَ النَّارَ عَلَى
الوَكِيلِ السَّابِقِ لِلْمَرَّةِ الثَّالِثَةَ عَشَرَةَ فَجَرَحَهُ.

78

٣ - يَحْوِي البَابُ الحَادِى وَالعِشْرُونَ عِلْمًا أَسَاسِيًّا
عَنِ السُّنَّةِ وَآرَاءِ الشِّيعَةِ عَنْها (فِيها) . ٤ - فِى أَوَائِلِ
القَرْنِ العِشْرِينَ ظَنَّ أَغْلَبِيَّةُ النَّاسِ الاِشْتِرَاكِيَّةَ نَوْعًا
مِنَ الشُّيُوعِيَّةِ. وَكَانَ ذَلِكَ أَحَدَ أَسْبَابِ عَــدَمِ
التَّوْفِيقِ (النَّجَاحِ) لِحِزْبِ العُمَّالِ فِى الاِنْتِخَابَاتِ
لِلْبَرْلَمَانِ. ٥ - مِن وَاجِبِ كُلِّ فَرْدٍ أَوَّلًا أَنْ يُؤْمِنَ كَمَا
آمَنَ المُسْلِمُونَ سَابِقًا ، وَثَانِيًا أَنْ يُصَلِّى صَلَوَاتِهِ
خَمْسَ مَرَّاتٍ يَوْمِيًّا ، وَثَالِثًا أَنْ يَتَوَكَّلَ عَلَى اللَّهِ ،
لِأَنَّ التَّوْفِيقَ مِنْهُ . ٦ - مَا هِىَ فَائِدَةُ مُنَافَشَةِ طَرِيقَةِ
فِى هَذِهِ الأَزْمَةِ ؟ قَد رَأَيْتَ (رَأَيْتُمْ) البَرْنَامِجَ الَّذِى
أُشِيعَ فِى مَجْلِسِ الأَمْنِ لِهَيْئَةِ الأُمَمِ المُتَّحِدَةِ .
٧ - أَنْتُمْ أَشْرَافٌ وَتَشَرَّفْنَا بِزِيَارَتِكُمْ ، فَإِنَّكُمْ شَرَّفْتُمُونَا
ثَلَاثَ تَشْرِيفَاتٍ ، بِمَجِيئِكُمْ ، وَبِهَدَايَاكُمُ النَّفِيسَةِ وَبِكَلِمَاتِكُمُ
اللَّطِيفَةِ . ٨ - رُفِعَ لِوَاءُ الاِسْتِقْلَالِ هُنَا أَمْسِ لِأَوَّلِ
مَرَّةٍ (لِلْمَرَّةِ الأُولَى) مُنْذُ أَوَاسِطِ القَرْنِ . ٩ - نَظَرَتْ

النِّسَاءَ إلى الهَدَايَا الَّتِي قد اسْتَلَمْنَهَا مِن أزْوَاجِهِنَّ
نَظَرَ الأطْفَالِ المَسْرُورِينَ ... ١٠- يَدَّعِي القُنْصُلُ أَنَّ هذا
المُرَاسِلَ يُرْسِلُ نِصْفَ الأخْبَارِ فَقَطْ، لٰكِنَّ رَأْيِي أنَّهُ لا
يُرْسِلُ أَكْثَرَ مِن رُبْعِهَا . ١١- والسَّبَبُ أنَّهُ يَقْضِي أرْبَعِينَ
فى المِائَةِ مِن وَقْتِهِ فى الأبْحَاثِ الخُصُوصِيَّةِ ولا يُفَكِّرُ فى
مُحْتَوَيَاتِ لِلجَرِيدَةِ الَّتِي يَشْتَغِلُ (يَعْمَلُ) فِيهَا . ١٢-"شَكْلٌ"
أسْمٌ مُفْرَدٌ . ١٣- الحَلُّ لِهٰذِهِ المَشْكِلَةِ ثُلاثِيٌّ . ١٤- قد قَرَأْتُ
كِتَابِي الألْفَ أثَرَ دُخُولِي فى المُسْتَشْفَى ، وهُوَ كِتَاب غَيْرُ
صَالِح (مُنَاسِبٍ) لِلأطْفَالِ . ١٥- كِدْتُ ألاَحِظُ التَّغْيِيرَ
فى ظُهُورِهِ (مَظْهَرِهِ) لَمَّا عَادَ (رَجَعَ) بَعْدَ غِيَابِ خَمْسٍ
وعِشْرِينَ سَنَةً . ١٦- عُمْرُهُ الآنَ سَبْعُونَ تَقْرِيبًا، لٰكِنَّكَ
إذا رَأيْتَهُ ظَنَنْتَهُ خَمْسِينَ، لا أكْثَرَ . ١٧- اِسْتَقَالَ ثُلُثُ
المُمَثِّلِينَ فى أثَرِ اسْتِلاَمِ (وُصُولِ) العَرِيضَةِ الأخِيرَةِ .
١٨- لٰكِنَّ السَّبَبَ الحَقِيقِيَّ هُوَ عَدَمُ الرَّأْسِمَالِ (رَأْسِ
المَالِ) لَدَى الشَّرِكَةِ . ١٩- قد قِيلَ لَهَا خَمْسَ مَرَّاتٍ

حَتَّى الآنَ أَنَّ هُناكَ أَمَلَ تَحْسِينِ الأَحْوالِ، لكِنَّهُمْ

بَيِسُوا مُنْذُ آسْتِقَالَةِ المُديرِ . ٢٠ ـ ذَاتَ يومٍ (فِي يومٍ

مِن الأَيَّامِ) قامَ رَجُلٌ عظِيمٌ مِن بَيْنِ النَّاسِ .

Exercise 73

1. The history of the Shi'ites goes back to the murder of
'Alī, who was the fourth Caliph; for his friends and helpers
hated the people responsible for this great crime. 2. You are
the only man who can carry out the necessary repairs to my
car, because of the length of your experience in work of this
sort. 3. Moreover (*lit.* add to that) all other workmen have
gone on strike, through hatred of the recent transfers.
4. They will only return to work on condition that they
participate in the management of the company. 5. Despair
filled the hearts of the sailors in the three fleets when news
reached them about the recent policy which had led to the
resignation of the war minister. 6. I am surprised at your
reading this long book so quickly. You have really tried
hard (*or* exerted yourself). 7. As for me, I am incapable of
reading like that, whatever circumstances might demand
(*lit.* whatever were the demands of circumstances). So do not
blame me. 8. Why are you running away, coward? When
will you recognise that hope is better than despair? 9. The
newspapers here were surprised at (some) foreign capitalists'
taking the nationality of the new republic. 10. When have
you decided to lead the army to fight the foe? 11. Have you
not heard that most of the fleet left port yesterday, and was
smashed on a rocky cape (*or* headland) near the capital?
12. You said "I will bring you tea", and I see that the word
"tea", though it came into the construction of your words,
did not at all come into the construction of this weak luke-
warm liquid! 13. Your writing is bad. Do you not know the

various shapes of the Arabic letters? Please write this page afresh in fine writing, otherwise you will not be transferred to a higher class! 14. He died a death of poverty after his continuous effort. 15. The accused rose, and said to the judge: "Your honour, my charge is of a kind unheard of up to now (*lit.* today)". 16. Three strikes have taken place this year. 17. I visited him while he was ill, lying on his bed like a dying man. 18. The guest said: "You are calling your servant. Do you not remember that you sent him to the market an hour ago to buy the requirements for the party?" 19. Look at those (*lit.* these) two! The husband is riding his camel, while his wife is walking at his side. 20. We are from God, and to him we shall return.

Exercise 74

١- إِنَّ الِاحْتِيَاجَ هوالمُعَلِّمُ الوَحِيدُ لِلرَّجلِ الَّذِي يَبْـذُلُ
دَرَاهِمَهُ . ٢- نَعرِفُ أَنَّ تَعْلِيمَاتٍ خَاصَّةً وَصَلَت عِدَّةَ
أَيَّامٍ قَبْلَ الإضْرَابِ الأَخِيرِ . ٣- نَقْلُ العَاصِمَةِ يَجْعَلُ مِنَ
الضَّرُورِيِّ (اللازِمِ) أيْضًا عِدَّةَ تَنَقُّلَاتٍ مُوَظَّفِينَ مِن مَكانٍ إلى
آخَرَ . ٤- كَرَاهِيَّتُكَ لذلك الرَّجلِ مَسْأَلَةُ الجِنْسِيَّةِ ،فَأَلُومُكَ
لَها ؛ ومع ذلك أُوَافِقُكَ أَنَّهُ رَجُلٌ ذُو خُلُقٍ سَيِّئٍ (رَجُلٌ
سَيِّئُ الأَخْلَاقِ) . ٥- تَأَسَّفْتُ مِن مَوْتِهِ لِأَنِّي أَعرِفُ أَنَّ تُهْمَتَهُ
غَيْرُ صَحِيحَةٍ . ٦- مَتَى يَعْتَرِفُ الرَّأْسَمَالِيُّونَ بِأَنَّ (أَنَّ)
دَفْعَ الأَجْرِ (الإيجَارَاتِ) العَالِيَةِ مِن أَهَمِّ أَسْبَابِ عَدَمِ

82

الثِّقَةِ بَيْنَ العُمَّالِ . ٧- كانت جَرِيمَتُهُ فَتْحَ مَكاتِيبَ

مَعْنُونَةٍ لِغَيْرِهِ بِخَطٍّ واضِحٍ . ٨- عَجِبْتُ مِنْ رِئاسَتِهِ

(قِيادَتِهِ) لِلأُسْطُولِ . وَنَشاطِهِ فى كُلِّ ما عَمِلَهُ أَثْناءَ

الحَرْبِ . ٩- كان إِعْطاؤُكَ إيّاهُ هذا المَبْلَغَ أَحَدَ شُرُوطِ

تَعْيِينِكَ . ١٠- أُضْرِبُ عَنْ عَمَلِكَ مُدَّةً قَصِيرَةً وَأَشْتَرِكُ

فى عِيدِنا إِكْرامًا لِعاداتِنا . ١١- قد رَكَّبْتَ لِلْجُمْلَةِ تَرْكِيبًا

جَمِيلًا (جَيِّدًا) . ١٢- هذا مِنْ أَىِّ نَوْعٍ هو مِنَ الرِّجالِ!

فَهَرَبَ هَرْبَةَ الجَبانِ ، ثُمَّ رَجَعَ كَأَنَّهُ بَجّارٌ مُنْتَصِرٌ . ١٣- مَتَى

تَعْرِفُ أَنّنا لا نَسْتَطِيعُ أَنْ نُكْرِهَ أَحَدًا كَراهِيَّةً مُطْلَقَةً؟

١٤- جاءَتِ الخادِماتُ سَرِيعًا بِمَآرِبْ دَتى ، وَوَضَعْنَ عَلَيْها

ثَلَاثَ كُتَّابِيّاتٍ سَائِلٍ فاتِرٍ أَخْضَرَ . ١٥- وكان مِن نَوْعٍ

لا يَكادُ يَشْرَبُهُ أَحَدٌ هُنا إِلّا الأَجانِبُ الجُهّالُ.

١٦- سَوْفَ أَقْبَلُ هذِه الخُطَّةَ بِشَرْطِ* أَنْ تُعْلِنَها ثَلَا ثَ ةَ

---

*Here شرط is definite (without *tanwin*) because the whole sentence
following is in a state of *iḍāfa* with it.

83

إِعْلَانَاتٍ : أَوَّلُهَا الْيَوْمَ وَالثَّانِي غَدًا وَالثَّالِثَ بَعْدَ أُسْبُوعٍ.

١٧- مَشَى مِشْيَةَ رَجُلٍ مُسِنٍّ. ١٨- إِنِّي خَارِجٌ (أَخْرُجُ)

لِأَنِّي لَا أُحِبُّ كَلَامَكَ. ١٩- أَقُولُ لَكَ هٰذَا لِئَلَّا تَلُومَنِي فِي

الْمُسْتَقْبَلِ. ٢٠- رَأَيْتُ أَوْلَادَكَ يَرْمُونَ (رَامِينَ) حَجَرًا

وَيُكَسِّرُونَ (مُكَسِّرِينَ) النَّوَافِذَ فِي بَيْتٍ جَارِي.

Exercise 75

(Bethlehem). I went from Jerusalem to the town of
Bethlehem, and I found en route (*or* on my way) 'Ain
Sulwān. This is the spring in which the Lord Christ cured
the blind man, who previously had no sight in either eye
(*lit.* he had not two eyes). Near it are many houses carved in
the rock. In them are (some) men who have incarcerated
themselves to worship (*or* out of piety). As for Bethlehem –
the place where Jesus Christ was born – between it and
Jerusalem is (a distance of) six miles. Half way along the
road is the tomb of Jacob's two sons. It is a tomb on which
are twelve stones. Over it is a dome vaulted with rock, and
Bethlehem is there. In it is a well-built church adorned to
the limit, so that there is not to be seen anything built thus
among all the churches (of the world). It is in a depressed
piece of land and has a gate on the West, and it has every
beauty of marble pillars. In a corner of the shrine to the
North is the cave in which Christ was born, and it is under-
neath the shrine. And in the cave is the manger in which
He was found. When you leave Bethlehem, you see in the
East the church of the angels who gave the shepherds the
good news of Christ's birth.

84

Exercise 76

١- أَتُّهِمَ أخي بِعِبَادَةِ الأَصْنَامِ خَارِجَ مَسْجِدِ عُمَرَ. ٢- لِهذِه الطُّيُورِ مَنَافِيذُ طَوِيلَةٌ. ٣- رَأَيْنَا عَيْنًا مِن ماءٍ صافٍ جارٍ خَارِجَ المَغَارَةِ. ٤- إنَّ قَبْرَ هُؤُلاءِ الرِجالِ على بُعْدِ أَرْبَعَةِ أَمْيَالٍ مِن المَكانِ الذِي حُبِسُوا فيه. ٥- إِذا طَلَبْتَ مِن مُدِيرِ المَخَازِنِ، أَعْطَاكَ ثَلَاثَةَ مَبَارِدَ ومِقَصًّا ومُدَقَّيْنِ، أَحَدُهُمَا كَبِيرٌ والثاني صَغِيرٌ. ٦- وَلَدَت قِطَّتِي السَّوْدَاءُ سَبْعَ قُطَيْطَاتٍ، إحْدَاهَا سَوْدَاءُ، وثَلاث مِنها شُهْبٌ، وبَيْضَاوَانِ، وسَمْرَاءُ. ٧- فِي رُكْنٍ مِن أَرْكَانِ هذا الهَيْكَلِ المُقَدَّسِ ثَلاثَةُ أَعْمِدَة مِن رُخَامٍ. ٨- رَأَت النِّساءُ قُبَّةً مَعْقُودَةً فِي وَسَطِ المَرَاعِي بِالقُرْبِ مِن البُحَيْرَةِ وعَرَفْنَ أَنَّه قَبْرُ يَعْقُوبَ. ٩- كُنْتُ أَخافُ مِن المَوْقِفِ غَايَةَ الخَوْفِ. ١٠- سَيَفْقِدُ سَنُ اسْمُهُ بَعِيدَ مَوْتِه.

١١- إنَّ بيتى مكانٌ للصَّلاةِ ، وقد جَعَلتُموهُ /تَشتَرى وتُباعُ فيها البَضائعُ . ١٢- كَنَستُ الحُجرةَ بِمِكنسةٍ جديدةٍ وكَوَيتَ مَلابِسى بِمِكوَةٍ جديد ، ومع ذلك عملُك ردىٌّ كُلُّهُ . ١٣- كان ميعادُنا للساعةِ الخامسةِ ، فلماذا لَمْ نصلْ حَتَّى الساعةِ السابعةِ ؟ ١٤- لندن مُلتَـــقَى للطُّلابِ من كلِّ أُمَّةٍ . ١٥- تُوجَدُ خارجَ مكتبى شُجَيرَةٌ فيها عِشُّ عندليبٍ . ١٦- بُعَيدَ الظُّهرِ يا بُنَّى سوف نَلتَقى فى جنينةٍ حسينٍ ، وفيها فواكهُ من أنواعٍ كثيرةٍ مختلفةٍ ، منها السَّفَرجَلُ والتفاحُ ، لكنى أُفَضِّلُ السفرجلَ . ١٧ - فتحتُ مكتبتهُ بالمفتاحِ ، ووجدتُ فيها مقالتهُ فى الاستقلالِ العربى ، وكانت بخطٍّ جيّدٍ . ١٨- العصفورُ طُيَيٌّ (طيرٌ صغيرٌ) معروفٌ فى انكلترا . ١٩- عَضَّــهُ عُقَيربٌ بينما كان يصلِّح المِرْوَحَة فى حجرةِ أخى . ٢٠- زِنْ كلَّ شىءٍ على (فى) المَوَازينِ الرسميةِ فى السوقِ فَلَيسَت لى ثِقَةٌ بِموازينِ التُّجّارِ .

86

Exercise 77

It is related (*lit.* has been related) that Hārūn al-Rashīd summoned one of his attendants called Ṣāliḥ. When he appeared before him, he said to him: "Ṣāliḥ, go to Manṣūr and say to him: You have 1,000,000 dirhams of ours, and opinion has prescribed that you bring (*lit.* carry) that sum to us this hour. I command you (*lit.* have commanded you), Ṣāliḥ, if you do not obtain that sum from now till sunset, you must take his head from his body, and bring it us." Ṣāliḥ said: "To hear is to obey."

Then he went to Manṣūr and mentioned to him what the Commander of the Faithful had informed him. Manṣūr said: "I am as good as dead (*lit.* I have perished). By heavens, my property and possessions if sold at the highest value would not exceed 100,000 in price. Where, Ṣāliḥ, can I obtain the remaining 900,000 dirhams?" Ṣāliḥ said to him: "Plan a trick with which to save yourself urgently, otherwise you will perish. For I cannot give you a moment's grace after the period specified to me by the Caliph. Be quick with a trick." Manṣūr said: "Ṣāliḥ, I ask you, please, to take me to my house to say good-bye to my children and family, and to give my last wishes to my relatives." Ṣāliḥ said: "Then I went with him to his house, and he began to say good-bye to his family. The clamour rose in his house, and the weeping, crying, and asking Almighty God's help were loud."

Exercise 78

١- وكان من بَيْنِ أَعْوَانِهِ مِصْرِيٌّ وإيطاليَانِ وَثلاثةٌ
من المَكِّيِّينَ المُسِنِّينَ قد لاقَاهُم فى حَجِّ السَّنَةِ السَّابِقَةِ

87

(الماضِيَةِ) * ٢- يُقالُ لِهذه المِنْطَقَةِ ٠ مِنطقةُ الصَّنائِع الخَفيفةِ ٠، وأنشأتْها الحكومةُ بَعْدَ أنَّ الحربَ قـد أزالَتْ جميعَ صنائعِ بلادِنا السابقةِ . ٣- قرأتُ فى يَوميّاتِهِ كيفَ خَلَّصَ نَفْسَهُ وكلَّ تعلُّقاتِه (كلُّ مـا يَمْلِك / يَمْلِكُهُ) بحيلةٍ . ٤- مِن فَضلِك أَرِنى (دُلَّنى على) الطريقَ لِلْمَطار المَدَنىّ . ٥- كان كلُّ شىءٍ غالِيًا فى انكلترا بعد الحرب . ٦- التعليمُ رَخيصٌ فى المدارس الثانَوية لِلحكومةِ الفَرَنْسِـيّةِ . ٧- الأكثَريّةُ أَوْمَسَتْ بتأميم جميع الشَّرِكاتِ التِّجاريّةِ ، فَعَلا (فَارْتَفَـعَ) صِياح و ضَجيج مِن الأقلية . ٨- ودَّعَنى زوجى لِآخِر مَرَّةٍ (لِلمَرَّةِ الأَخِيرةِ) ، فأستغِيثُ باللهِ تعالى فى مَشاكلى الصعبة . ٩- الإخطاءُ مِن الإنسان والمَغفِرةُ مِن اللهِ **
١٠- زادتْ شُهرةُ العُمّالِ أثرَ اتِّفاقيّةٍ (اتِّفاق) بَيْنَهُم وبين

---

* The translation means literally "in the pilgrimage of the former (past) year".

** See the Grammar, Vocabulary p. 616 under غفر .

المُسْتَخْدِمِين. ١١- الصِّحَة الروحانية أَهُمُّ من الصحة الجُسْمانِية. ١٢- إِنِّي رجل محبوب ولستُ سريعاً للغَضب.

١٣- قابَلتُ سائلاً فى الشارع – وقد كان تجاراً سابِقًا فقال: إِنِّي فقيرٌ مسكينٌ، فأعطني شيئًا. ١٤- قلتُ: لَيْسَ معى من دراهمَ، فاستغِثْ باللهِ تعالى. ١٥- هو كان عَلَّامة وأكثرُ اجتهادًا من العلماء الآخرين.

١٦- يا بُنَّى إِنَّ وجهَك أسود كالفحم فأَيْنَ كُنْتَ؟

١٧- الجامعة أكبر اليوم منها (مِمَّا كانت) سابِقًا.

١٨- هم أحسنُ فى العمل منهم فى الكلِمات (الكلام).

١٩- كانت كَلِماتُها أحلى من السُّكَّر، لكِنَّ أفكارَها مُرَّةٌ كَالخَلِّ. ٢٠- أنتم رجال دُنْيَوِيُّونَ جِدًّا. ٢١- إِنَّ عَبْقَرِيَّةَ عُمَرَ مشهورةٌ فى تأريخ الخلفاء.

Exercise 79

A

As for Abū l-Ḥasan ibn Naṣr, known as al-Qirmīsīnī, the grammarian, he studied under (*lit.* took from) ʿAlī ibn Sulaimān al-Akhfashī. ʿAbd al-Salām ibn Ḥusain al-Baṣrī studied under him. Ibn Abū al-Fawāris said: The grammarian ʿAlī ibn Hārūn al-Qirmīsīnī died in (the month of) Jumādā al-ʿĀkhira in 371, during the caliphate of al-Ṭāʾī. He said: "He had from Abū Ḥasan al-ʿAkhfash many things", and I heard him say: "He was a fine reliable authority, and was born in 290."

B

1. What is the meaning of meanness and generosity? The former is the opposite of the latter, for the former is a vice and the latter a virtue, since (both) the religions of Islam and Christianity demand that a man give. The fortunate man who has more than sufficient must be concerned about the unfortunate, and give them enough to live on. This is a príncìple, in both religions, of great importance, and this fundamental principle has had great influence in human history. 2. In that discussion one of the members claimed that the telegram contained important news of the recent negotiations. 3. This poet was given the nickname "Taʿabbaṭa Sharran" because he was carrying a ghoul under his arm one day. But I consider this story an untrue legend unworthy of the reader's consideration. 4. Poetry is an art, and the poet is an artist in words. In the Arab view, poetry is the greatest literary art. 5. What is the leader's point of view on the necessary measures? Has he not replied to the telegram? When will an announcement be made on the question? 6. I had the greatest luck (*or* good fortune), since I discovered silver and other metals in the southern province. 7. You will have the chance to take another look at the girl from that high window, and that is sufficient for a young man like you.

Exercise 80

A

إنّ مَعْنَى البخلِ ان الرجلَ يريـد ان ينخذ كل شــــئ
لنفســه ولا يُحِبُّ أن يعطى لغيره . وهو من أكبر
الرذائل فى الاســلام والنَصْرانيّة (المَسِيحِيّة) على
السواء . وعكسُـه الكَرمُ ،الذى كان أكبَر فضيلةٍ
عند العرب (البـدو) فى الجاهِلِيّة . وهناك كنـاب
مشهور عن (فى) البخل اسـمه (عنوانه) «كتاب
البخلاء » وهو لِلجاحِظ ، الذى عاش فى القرن التاسع
وآمُلُ أن تكون لك فرصةُ قِرَاءتِه ، لأنه كتاب ذو أهمية
عظيمة فى تأريخ الآداب العربية وهو كتاب عظيم
حتى من وجهة نظر الأوربيين . ومن لا يعرف العربية
يستطيع أن يقرأه فى ترجمة فرنسية حسنة. وإنّه
يحوى حكايات رِجال كثيرين فى ولايات الدولة الإسلامية
المختلفة .

B

يا قارئُ، لعلّك من بين أُولئُك الطلاب البخيتين

91

الذين يهتمون بالشعر العربي . فالشعر أقدمُ فنونِ العرب .

ومَبَادِئُهُ ما كادت تتغيّر أثناء مدّة ثلاث عشرة مائة/ سنة

وكان العربُ القدماءُ يحكون روايات (حكايات) كثيرة

عن شعرائهم . وتُوجَدُ أسطورةٌ عجيبةٌ عن الشاعر المشهور،

'تأبّطَ شَرًّا، فيُقالُ إنه خرج فى الصحراء ، فى يوم من

الأيام ولاقَى غُولاً ـ أى نوع من الشيح ـ هناك. فحمَلَهُ

الشاعر تحت ابطه إلى بيته وأخاف أقرباءه. وبَعْدَ

هذا الحادث لُقّبَ بـ«تأبّطَ شَرًّا » .

c

١- الذهب والفضّة معدنان نفيسان ، ويجىء كثير

من ذهبنا من افريقيا الجنوبية . ٢- سُمِعَ بلاغٌ أنّ

المناورات بين الجانبين قد نَجَحَتْ . ٣- أُجَبْتُ عليه

بيرقية (بتلغراف) أنّى سوف أتخذ الإجراءات/ ٤- ذكر
                                     اللازمة

أثناء المناقشات أنّ نافذتين لا تُكْفِيانِ حتى لأصغر

حجرةٍ فى البيت . ٥- اشتكى زعيمهم من علو الكرسى الذى

92

كان الرئيسُ يجلس (جالساً) عليه ، وقال: إنه يجلس
جلسةَ أميرٍ شرقيٍّ (يجلس مثل أميرٍ/كأمير شرقيٍّ).

٦- هذه مسألة ذات أهمية كبيرة للحكومة.

Exercise 81
Death of the kings of Ceylon

When the king dies in the land of Ceylon, he is placed on a
carriage near the ground, hung on its rear end lying on his
back, while his hair (*lit.* the hair of his head) drags along the
dust on the ground. A woman with a broom in her hand
pours dust on his head, and cries: "Oh people, this was your
king yesterday, ruling you, and effective among you. Through
quitting the world he has become what you (now) see. The
angel of death has taken his soul. So do not, after him, be
beguiled by life." Such words (are spoken) during three
days. Then sandalwood, camphor and saffron are prepared
for him and he is burned, and his ashes thrown to the wind.
The Indians all burn their dead with fire. Ceylon is the last
of the islands, and it is part of the land of India (*or* the
Indians). And sometimes (when) the king is burned, his
wives enter the fire and are burned with him.

Exercise 82
A

اغترّ الناس بالكِبرياء ، فَعَمّ الفَوْضاء ، وكل يوم نسـمعُ
فَوضى في شوارع العاصمة ، ويشرب الشبابُ الخمرَ
فيسكرون، فيجرون من دكان إلى دكان (إلى آخِر)

93

وإنهم ، حتى الآن، قد أحرقوا أكثر من مائة دكان .
وكسـر ولد واحد – ورُبّما عمره نحو عشـر سـنوات –
نوافذ عدّة دكاكين بفأس صغيرة . وإذا كان هذا روحَ
القوميةِ الجديدَ (للجديدةَ) فإنّي أفضّل الدُوليّةَ.

B

غَرّتني الهندُ أثناء الحرب الأخيرة . فخدمتُ في الجيشِ
الهندى مع الجنودِ الهنودِ ، لكني رأيتُ أيضًا الكثيرَ
(كثيرًا) من المناظرِ العجيبة لتلك البلادِ الجميلة ؛وبعضُ
أقسـامها مثلِ فِرْدَوس لِمَنْ يحبُّ الألوانَ والأضواءَ . لكنَّ
فيها زيادةَ سـكانٍ ، وكثيرٌ منهم فقراء جدًا ، وللحكومة الجديدة
الوطنية تكافِحُ الفقر بنشـاطٍ عظيمٍ . وأملي أن تنجحَ .

C

احترقَ بيتُ رئيسِ الوزراءِ اليومَ بعد الظُهرِ، وما وصلت
فرقةُ المطافئ إلّا بعد أربع ساعات . وسببُ ذلك ات
سـيارتِها بحالٍ سـيئة فانكسرت اثنان منها وكانتا
94

تنتظران التصليح . وكان (كانت)* من بين الذين ماتوا

فى الحريق أُمُّ رئيسِ الوزراءِ المُسِنَّةُ وزوجتُه الثانيةُ

الحُبْلَى (الحامل) .

D

وجدتُ سارقًا (لِصًّا) فى البيت فى الليل وما كانت معى

بندقية ولا سلاح آخر، فضربتهُ على عنقه بكأس من

فِضَّة قد كسبتُها (ربحتها) لمّا ركبتُ فى سباق الخيل .

ولمّا رأى الدكتورُ السارقَ قال إنه أصبح غيرَ مسرورٍ

لأنّ زوجته عاقرٌ، وكان ذلك سبب التجائِه إلى حياة

الإجرام . أمّا زوجتى فهى امرأةٌ صبورٌ جدا لكنها لا تصدّق

كل هذه الأفكار (الآراء) الجديدة التى دخلت فى علم الطبّ

فتقول: " ليس هذا الرجل مريضًا . إنّه مُجرِمٌ لكنّ هـذه

الكلمةَ قبيحةٌ ولا يحبّ الناسُ الكلماتِ القبيحةَ (فى) هذه

* The preceding verb, being separated from its following subject,
may be put in the masculine, even though that subject is feminine.
This usage was permitted, though by no means universal. It is
sometimes found in present-day Arabic.

الأيام ، وإن كانت حَقيقيَّة . إنَّ داءَ هذا الرجل هى

السرقُ والدواءُ الملائم(المناسب) هو السجنُ » .

Exercise 83

A

Brethren, know that whosoever does good in his (*lit.* the)
days, his affairs are blessed. Whoever does evil in them has
wasted (*lit.* lost) his life. He who has fallen short shall
tomorrow regret his falling short. He who neglects (*lit.*
leaves) work for his future will regret this. He who abandons
guidance after being enlightened shall weep. For the days of
one's life are days of haste which (soon) go, and the seizing
of days which are taken away (from one). So hasten with your
life before you depart, and profit by your life before you die.

B

A just government is not sufficient to those people. They
hasten to self-determinations and self-government as the
rest of the peoples of this continent have done. Their aim is
not to miss the chance (*lit.* not to let the opportunity pass
them). Yes! They seize the opportunity, and strive to
deserve independence.

C

1. Open your lips for me to see your teeth. 2. How did the
pot break, and it was in your hands a minute ago? Take a
firm hold of these pots, in the hope that they will not fall
from your hand. 3. The journey of Ibn Baṭṭūṭa from India
to China is famous. At the beginning, the infidels (*or* unbelievers) seized him, but he escaped from them. Finally, he
reached China after strenuous efforts. 4. The standard of
living in Europe rose (*lit.* was raised) to an unforeseen level (*or*

extent, degree). 5. Praise be to God the Lord of the Worlds*.
6. I have great difficulty with names of Muslims, as I find
half of them are Muḥammads! 7. They met four white
women of great beauty†. 8. This tool has many different
uses. 9. Death took the governor of the Northern province,
and he left three sons and four daughters. 10. I saw many
spiders in the pashas' and beys' rooms, so sweep (*addressed
to a female*) all the rooms afresh.

Exercise 84

A

تَعَاوَنَ المُحَمَّدُونَ الثَّلَاثَةُ (.mod الثَّلَاثَةُ مُحَمَّدِينَ)

فى اقْتِرَافِ هٰذِهِ الجَرِيمَةِ ، ثُمَّ نَدِمَ الأَوَّلَانِ عَلَيْهَا وعَفَوْتُ

عَنْهُمَا . أَمَّا الثَّالِثُ فَلَا أَعْرِفُ مَاذَا يَكُونُ المَصِيرُ .

فإنَّهُ لَيْسَ ابنَ أَبَوَيْنِ فَقِيرَيْنِ ، إِنَّمَا أَبُوهُ وعَمُّهُ غَنِيَّانِ

وبُعْطِيَاهُ كُلَّ مَا يَطْلُبُهُ ، لٰكِن يَظْهَرُ أَنَّهُ يَقْرَأُ رِوَايَاتِ

الجَرَائِمِ لِلْكُتَّابِ الأُورُبِّيِّينَ العَصْرِيِّينَ ويَغْتَنِمُ كُلَّ فُرْصَةٍ

لِلسَّرِقِ والمُقَاتَلَةِ ، فَتَخَافُ المَدِينَةُ مِنْهُ كُلُّها . ولَا

يَسْتَطِيعُ أَبُوهُ أَنْ يَفْعَلَ شَيْئًا بِهِ . وَقَبَضَهُ عَلَيْهِ

---

* Interpreted by some as "Lord of Mankind".

† حُسْن and جَمَال both mean "beauty", and their juxtaposition is for
stress. Thus they can be translated by using the adjective "great".
Otherwise, they can be translated by two synonyms such as "beauty
and loveliness".

97

البوليس (الشُّرْطة) سبع مرّات أثناء الأشهر السبعة الماضية. وإنّي آملُ أن نجد عملًا نافعًا لاجتهادانه في المستقبل وأن يُصبح عضوًا مفيدًا للمُجْتَمَع.

B

لا تكادُ هؤلاء البنات يَفْتَحْنَ أَفْوَاهَهُنَّ حين يتكلمن. أفانَتَهُنَّ أن الوضوح أهمّ شيء في الكلام؟ هن هندات كلهن، ويُرِدْنَ كلهن أن يُصبحن كاتبات. ويَسْعينَ جِدّ المساعي لِيَصِلْنَ مستوًى عاليًا في دراستهن وفضلةً عن كلامهن قد نَجَحْنَ نجاحًا واسعًا في علمهن.

C

١- ما هو قصدُكَ (ما هي نِيَّتُكَ) من هذه الرِّحْلة الطويلة الصعبة؟ ليس في الدنيا مكانٌ لم يَزُرْهُ مسافرٌ من المسافرين، وأنت كبير السن. فأستحسن أن تبقى في بيتك وتترك كل هذه المساعي لغيرك.

٢- مسك الآنية ووضعها كلها على الأرض. ثم كسرها

98

قصدًا بآلةٍ غريبةٍ ثقيلةٍ . ٣ ـ أنتم كُلّكُم آغـوات

وباشوات فى نظر الجمهوريين ، مهما كنتم ســابقًا ،

فلاحين أو أُمراء .

Exercise 85

A

Perspiration was flowing on the man's forehead when he saw the wild boar (*or* pig). For he had no protection. In that moment he thought of his young son who would become an orphan if he himself died, and of his wife who would become a weeping widow. Then suddenly the boar stopped, so the man began to run across the sand. He left the place as fast as possible, until he reached a house and entered it.

B

1. Russia colonised most of northern Asia during the nineteenth century. 2. I found that my serving girl has eaten all the oranges, and I saw no means of buying more fruit. 3. The minister read next year's (*or* the following year's) budget, and did not like it (*or* was not pleased with it). 4. The criminal was taken into custody (*or* arrested) and all the people recommended that he be executed (*lit.* his execution).

Exercise 86

١ ـ إِنتَهَتْ دُنْيَاى بَعْدَ أَن أَصبحَتُ أَرملةً ، فلمّا بلغتُ

من عُمرى إحدى عتشرة سنة توفّى أبى . وقد ماتت أمى

قبل هذا بثلاث سنين . ٢ ـ نرى فى ميزانية روسيا مبالغَ

99

ضَخْمَةً للدفاع عن حدودها . ٣- إنّ مساعدة الأرامِلِ

وهُدَاهُنَّ من بين الواجبات المقترح بها على المؤمنين .

٤- كانت له خنازيرُ كثيرةٌ فضلاً عن بقرٍ وضأنه . ٥- قَابَلَ

بنتاً سوداء فاستخدمها خادمةً في بيته ببغداد، لكنها

هَجَرَتْهُ فجأةً بدون إذن بعد يومين . ٦- لَحِقُوا الأعداء

ووجدوهم يتوقّفون (متوقّفين) في الرمل فأعدموهم حالاً .

٧- كانت لِلبُرْتُغال مستعمراتٌ كثيرةٌ في الماضى وكان

بُحَّارُوها مشهورين . ٨- عرفتُ من العرق السائل عـلـى

جبينه أنّ مساعيه/أتْعَبَتْهُ قد ولكن هذا كان طريقتى

الوحيدة لإتمام العمل عند ميعاده . ٩- رأيتُ محمّدًا

على يسارى وأحمد على يمينى، أما طرفة المتكبّر فلَمْ أرَهُ

قط، فقد تركنى في وقت شِدَّتى . ١٠- لَقَيْتُ رجلاً

أعرج، وأسود طويلا في الشارع ولا أعرف من أين جاءا.

Exercise 87

One day ‘Umar ibn al-Khaṭṭāb went out wandering in the
market and was met by Abū Lu’lu’a, who was a Christian.

He said: "Oh Commander of the Faithful, I have a heavy poll-tax." He (i.e. 'Umar) said: "How much is your poll-tax?" He (Abū Lu'lu'a) said: "Two dirhams daily." He said: "What is your occupation?" He said: "A carpenter, engraver, and blacksmith." He ('Umar) said: "Then I do not consider your poll-tax excessive (*lit.* great) according to the jobs you do. I have heard that you say: If I wanted to make a windmill, I could (*lit.* I would do)." He said: "Yes". He said: "Then make me a mill." He said: "If you are preserved, I will indeed make you a mill about which those in the East and the West will talk." Then he left him. Then 'Umar said: "The slave (*or* servant) has threatened me previously." Then 'Umar went off home. On the next day, Ka'b al-'Aḥbār came to him and said: "Oh Commander of the Faithful, you will be dead in three days. " He said: "How do you know (*lit.* what tells you)?" He said: "I find it in God's book, the Pentateuch." 'Umar said: "Fear God! Then you find 'Umar ibn al-Khaṭṭāb in the Pentateuch?" He said: "No, but I find your description, and your fixed term of life has come to an end." Now 'Umar did not feel any ache or pain. Next day, Ka'b came to him, and said: "Oh Commander of the Faithful, one day has gone, and two remain (*lit.* have remained)." Then he came to him the day after that and said: "Two days have gone, and a day and night remain." When dawn came 'Umar went out to prayer, and Abū Lu'lu'a entered with the people, with a two-pointed dagger in his hand, with its handle in the middle. He struck 'Umar six blows, one of them beneath his navel, and that was the one that killed him. There was also killed, with him, Kulaib ibn Abī al-Bukair al-Laithī who was behind him. When 'Umar felt the heat of the weapon he fell down and said: "Is 'Abd al-Raḥmān ibn 'Auf among the people?" They said: "Yes, Commander of the Faithful, there he is!" He said: "Come forward, and lead the people in prayer (*lit.* pray with the people)." So 'Abd al-Raḥmān ibn 'Auf prayed, while 'Umar was prostrate. Then 'Umar was taken into his house.

خَرَجَ عُمَرُ بْنُ ٱلْخَطَّابِ يَوْمًا يَطُوفُ فِي ٱلسُّوقِ فَلَقِيَهُ أَبُو لُؤْلُؤَةٍ، وَكَانَ نَصْرَانِيًّا، فَقَالَ: يَا أَمِيرَ ٱلْمُؤْمِنِينَ إِنَّ عَلَيَّ خَرَاجًا كَثِيرًا.

قَالَ: وَكَمْ خَرَاجُكَ؟ قَالَ: دِرْهَمَانِ فِي كُلِّ يَوْمٍ. وَقَالَ: أَيْشَ (أَيُّ شَيْءٍ) صِنَاعَتُكَ؟ قَالَ: نَجَّارٌ وَنَقَّاشٌ وَحَدَّادٌ. فَقَالَ (عُمَرُ) فَمَا أَرَى خَرَاجَكَ بِكَثِيرٍ عَلَى مَا تَصْنَعُ مِنَ ٱلْأَعْمَالِ. قَدْ بَلَغَنِي أَنَّكَ تَقُولُ: لَوْ أَرَدْتُ أَنْ أَعْمَلَ رَحًى تَطْحَنُ بِالرِّيحِ فَعَلْتُ.

قَالَ: نَعَمْ. قَالَ: فَاعْمَلْ لِي رَحًى. قَالَ: لَئِنْ سَلِمْتُ لَأَعْمَلَنَّ لَكَ رَحًى يَتَحَدَّثُ بِهَا (عَنْهَا) مَنْ بِالْمَشْرِقِ وَٱلْمَغْرِبِ. ثُمَّ ٱنْصَرَفَ عَنْهُ. فَقَالَ عُمَرُ: لَقَدْ تَوَعَّدَنِي ٱلْعَبْدُ آنِفًا. ثُمَّ ٱنْصَرَفَ عُمَرُ إِلَى مَنْزِلِهِ. فَلَمَّا كَانَ مِنَ ٱلْغَدِ (لَمَّا كَانَ ٱلْغَدُ) جَاءَهُ كَعْبُ ٱلْأَحْبَارِ فَقَالَ، يَا أَمِيرَ ٱلْمُؤْمِنِينَ إِنَّكَ مَيِّتٌ فِي ثَلَاثَةِ أَيَّامٍ.

قَالَ: وَمَا يُدْرِيكَ؟ قَالَ: أَجِدُهُ فِي كِتَابِ ٱللهِ ٱلتَّوْرَاةِ. قَالَ عُمَرُ: اللهَ إِنَّكَ لَتَجِدُ عُمَرَ بْنَ ٱلْخَطَّابِ فِي ٱلتَّوْرَاةِ؟ قَالَ: لَا وَلَكِنِّي أَجِدُ

مِبْفَتَكَ وَإِنَّهُ قَدْ نَفَى أَجَلَكَ . وَعُمَرُ لَا يُحِسُّ وَجَعًا وَلَا أَلَمًا .

فَلَمَّا كَانَ ٱلْغَدُ جَاءَهُ كَعْبٌ فَقَالَ : يَا أَمِيرَ ٱلْمُؤْمِنِينَ، ذَهَبَ

يَوْمٌ وَبَقِيَ يَوْمَانِ . ثُمَّ جَاءَهُ مِنْ غَدِ ٱلْغَدِ ، فَقَالَ : ذَهَبَ يَوْمَانِ

وَبَقِيَ يَوْمٌ وَلَيْلَةٌ فَلَمَّا كَانَ ٱلصُّبْحُ خَرَجَ عُمَرُ إِلَى ٱلصَّلَاةِ وَدَخَلَ

أَبُو لُؤْلُؤَةٍ فِي ٱلنَّاسِ، فِي يَدِهِ خِنْجَرٌ لَهُ رَأْسَانِ، نِصَابُهُ

فِي وَسَطِهِ، فَضَرَبَ عُمَرَ سِتَّ ضَرَبَاتٍ، إِحْدَاهُنَّ تَحْتَ

سُرَّتِهِ وَهِيَ ٱلَّتِي قَتَلَتْهُ وَقُتِلَ مَعَهُ كُلَيْبُ بْنُ أَبِي ٱلْبُكَيْرِ

ٱللَّيْثِيُّ وَكَانَ خَلْفَهُ ، فَلَمَّا وَجَدَ عُمَرُ حَرَّ ٱلسِّلَاحِ سَقَطَ

وَقَالَ : أَفِي ٱلنَّاسِ عَبْدُ ٱلرَّحْمَانِ بْنُ عَوْفٍ ؟ فَالُوا : نَعَمْ يَا

أَمِيرَ ٱلْمُؤْمِنِينَ ، هُوَ ذَا . قَالَ : تَقَدَّمْ فَصَلِّ بِٱلنَّاسِ . فَصَلَّى

عَبْدُ ٱلرَّحْمَانِ بْنُ عَوْفٍ ، وَعُمَرُ طَرِيحٌ ثُمَّ أُدْخِلَ دَارُهُ .

Exercise 89

A

Ḥasan took up writing as a profession (*lit.* the profession of
writing) since his youth, when he left the intermediate
school. But he has no writings in the true sense (of the word),

and he has reached the age of 60 now. The reason for that is his laziness because he spent his time eating, drinking and playing. He has written a number of booklets and articles in the daily papers. He has told me himself, while drunk, that he did not justify the hopes of his parents and teachers; and that he was very sad about his failure at first, then he got used to it. We have all seen men like him who have failed in their work, despite their outstanding qualifications. Indeed, we may have given them salutary and useful advice, and they have not listened to us.

B

1. Go to my room, and bring me the book that I borrowed from the library the day before yesterday. 2. Stand behind him, and pay attention out of respect for the preacher. 3. The climate in Bahrein is hotter than in Syria, and that doubtless increases the difficulty of life in that island. 4. Our life is short and death is inevitable in the end, so let us do works with which God will be pleased, so that we may be worthy of preservation in the next world. 5. I saw both of them approaching, and I had called two other servants.

C

1. It was your brother Zaid himself who went off when the prince arrived. 2. They asked for food, so I gave it them, then they returned the following day with the same request, so I refused. 3. I saw a boy crossing the road while there was a great deal of traffic in it, so I called: "Watch out for the vehicles!" So he began to run till he reached the other side. 4. I was surprised that there was no alternative to taking refuge with the desert Arabs. 5. We corresponded with each other over a period of 50 years. 6. I passed beautiful (*or* fine) animals which belonged to a caravan halted under the trees.

١- على الرُّغم مِن قَولِ الكُنَّارِ، فإنّ أَرواحَ الصالحينَ في يَدِ
اللهِ. ٢- دَهِشتُ مِن أَنَّهُ لا شيءُ في العِقابِ بعد الخَلةِ.
ولا شكَّ (في) أن المُقَدَّمَةَ أكلوا كل ما بَقى. لكِن ماذا أعمل؟
هذه هِى العادة العامّة بين خِدمة موظفى الحكومة، فلابُدَّ
منها. ٣- إنْ ذهبتُ إلى القصر لأُقدّمَ عرضَحالى في الصبح
يقولوا إنّ الملك لا يزال نائماً، وإذا ذهبت بعد الظهر
قالوا إنه خرج إلى الصيد؛ وإذا ذهبت في المساء قالوا
إنه يستقبل الضيوف من السفراء والأجانب الآخرين
المهمين. ولا فائدة من هذا النوع من الحُكم. ٤- أَدهَشَنى
لأنه كان يقرأ مجلدات ضخمة، ولا يزال في شبابه. ٥- إيّاه
أمدح لكن إيّاك أستعين، لأنك كُنتَ صديقى منذ
طفولتى. ٦- رَفَضتُ أن أزورَه، قائلًا ان الطقس ردىء،
ولكنه كان أكثر ذكاءً مِن أن يصدّقنى. والسبب الحقيقى

انه كان رفض أن يقبل نصيحتى أنا. ٧- ما كانت مؤهلاته كافيةً لمثل هذه الحرفة. فكُنّا فى نفس الفصل فى المدرسة. وكان المعلم يتوقع أشياء كبيرة من كِلَيْنَا. لكنه كان يلهو بينما أشتغل أنا، وقلما انتبه لما قاله المعلم فى الدروس. وقَدْ تقول : " رُبّ رجلٍ نجح فى الحياة بدون مؤهلات كثيرة ". لكن كم نجحوا بدون عمل؟

٨- كم دراهمَ سَلَّفْتَهُ؟ رأيْنه، وهوسكران، قبل خمس دقائق، مع أنّهُ مفلس. ٩- تحادثوا وبعد فوات مدة قصيرة كانوا يتقاتلون. ١٠- مررت بك ماشيًا مع أُختى ليلةَ أَمس. أيعرف أبى ذلك؟ وهَلْ مِن نِيَّتِكَ أن تخطبها؟ أنا أخشى انه ليس لك أمل. لا شكّ فى أن أبى سيرفض تزويجها بك، لأنّ فتىً مثلك لا يستطيع أن يعطيها ما اعتادته من أشياء ونصيحتى إليك هى أن تبذلَ جهدك لتصبحَ غنيًا. ثم لعلك تحصل على موافقة أبى على الزواج .

It is said (*lit.* it has been said) that two thieves stole a donkey and one of them went to sell it. He was met by (*the active of the Arabic is turned into the passive*) a man who had a tray of fish, who said to him: "Will you sell this donkey?" He said: "Yes". He said: "Take this tray, so that I can ride it and test it, and if I like it I will buy it at a price which will be very satisfactory to you." So the thief took the tray, and the man mounted the donkey, and began to make it gallop (*lit.* run) to and fro, until it was far away from the thief. Then he entered a side street, till he was quite out of his sight (*lit.* concealed from him completely). The man was perplexed at that, and ultimately realised that it was a trick against him. So he went back with the tray and his companion met him. He said: "What have you done with the donkey? Have you sold it?" He said: "Yes". He said: "For how much?" He said: "For what it cost, and this tray is profit!"

Exercise 92

قِيلَ أَنْ لِصَّيْنِ سَرَقَا حِمَارًا وَمَضَى أَحَدُهُمَا لِيَبِيعَهُ .

فَقَابَلَهُ رَجُلٌ مَعَهُ طَبَقٌ فِيهِ سَمَكٌ فَقَالَ لَهُ : أَتَبِيعُ هٰذَا

الْحِمَارَ ؟ قَالَ : نَعَمْ . قَالَ : أَمْسِكْ هٰذَا الطَّبَقَ حَتَّى أَرْكَبَهُ

وَأُجَرِّبَهُ ، فَإِنْ أَعْجَبَنِي اشْتَرَيْتُهُ بِثَمَنٍ يُعْجِبُكَ . فَأَمْسَكَ

اللِّصُّ الطَّبَقَ وَرَكِبَ الرَّجُلُ الْحِمَارَ ، وَأَخَذَ يُجْرِيهِ نَهَابًا

وَإِيَابًا حَتَّى ابْتَعَدَ عَنِ اللِّصِّ كَثِيرًا . فَدَخَلَ بَعْضَ الْأَزِقَّةِ

وَآخْتَفَى عَنْهُ بِٱلْكُلِّيَّةِ . وَأَخَذَتِ ٱللُّصَّ ٱلْحَيْرَةُ مِنْ ذٰلِكَ

وَعَرَفَ أَخِيرًا أَنَّهَا حِيلَةٌ عَلَيْهِ . فَرَجَعَ بِٱلطَّبَقِ فَٱلْتَقَاهُ

رَفِيقُهُ فَقَالَ : مَا فَعَلْتَ بِٱلْحِمَارِ؟ هَلْ بِعْتَهُ؟ قَالَ : نَعَمْ .

قَالَ : بِكَمْ ؟ قَالَ : بِرَأْسِ مَالِهِ . وَهٰذَا ٱلطَّبَقُ رِبْحٌ !

Exercise 93

So he obtained (*lit.* took) for them light food, appetising and
tasty, which did not cost much. When they had eaten it and
washed their hands, he approached them and said: "I ask
you in the name of God, than whom nothing is greater, am
I now (*lit.* the hour) in easier circumstances and richer than
I was before you ate my food?" They said: "We do not
doubt that you were richer and in easier circumstances when
the food was in your possession." He said: "Then am I now
nearer to poverty, or was I then?" They said: "But of course
you are nearer to poverty now." He said: "Then who can
blame me for failing to invite people who bring me nearer to
poverty and take me further away from wealth? The more I
invite them the nearer I am to poverty, and the further I am
from wealth."

Exercise 94

١- قابلته يمشى ببطء على ضفة النهر ، يأخذ(يخطو)

خطوات قصيرة ، فسألت:من أَيْنَ جاء هذا الرجل

الغريب ولماذا يمشى بحزن كأنَّ جميع هموم الدنيا

على كِتِفَيْهِ ؟ فهل أدعوه إلى بيتي ، لأني رجل غنــى ، فأعطيه طعامًا مليحًا شـهـيًّا ؟ وعندما يترك بيــتى لعله (ربّما) يكون أسعد مما كان قَبْلُ .

ناديتُه ، لكنه لم يسمعنى ولا يُجيبُ . وبدا (ظهر) كَأَنَّمَا ظنونه الخصوصية أهمّ من أن يهتمّ بِسَارٍ ، فناديته مرّة ثانية بصوت عالٍ ، وَٱلْتَفَتَ إِلَيَّ عابسًا .

تردَّد قليلا ، ثم قال بغضب : « أقابلتك قبلُ ؟ أتعرفنى ؟ » قُلْتُ : « لا ، لكنى افتكرت أنك ربما كُنْتَ فى الضيق ، فأَرَدْتُ أن أساعدك . هل تجيئُ عندى (إلى بيتى) ؟ ونستريح هناك هُنَيْهَةً وتأكل وتشرب شـيئًا معى ؟ »

فأجاب : « يقولون إنّ بيت الانكليزى قصرٌ ، لكنك أنت تريد أن تجعل بيتك فندقًا أو بيت الفقراء أو ملجأَ الأيتام . أتظنُّ أن غريبًا مثلك يستطيع أن

يساعدني؟ اسمح لى بأن أعطيك نصيحة وان لم
تسمع ، أعطيتها . اذهب فى حالك !»

فانصرف ، واستمررت فى طريقى .

وفى اليوم التالى قرأت فى الجريدة المحلية أنّ جُثَّةَ
رجل مجهول قد وُجِدَتْ فى النهر . وانه قد غرق واله ليس
سبب ظاهر لذلك . وحتى الآن لا أعرف أهو الرجل الذى
قد لاقيته الذى غرق ، أم غيره . لكنى دائماً أتصور
أن هموم ذلك الرجل الفقير المسكين العابس أصبحت
أثقل من أن يَحْتَمِلَهَا ، فانتحر بالنطّ فى النهر . وأحياناً
أسأل نفسى : أ كان فى اسْتِطَاعَتى أن أخلّصَه ؟

Exercise 95

There has been dispute about the shape of the seas. Most
ancient philosophers of India, and Greek sages, apart from
those who disagreed with them and agreed with what the
sharī‘a experts say, take the view that the sea is circular in
the various places of the earth. They adduce many proofs for
the truth of that, including the fact that if you continue on
the sea, the earth and mountains disappear bit by bit until
they have all disappeared, and you see nothing of mountain
peaks. Then if you approach the coast, those mountains
come into view bit by bit, and trees and land appear.

١- وَلِّ واتِّجه لِي، لأني استللتُ سيفى ولا أريدُ أن

أضربَ رجلاً فى ظهره. ٢- لجَّ فى دراسته الشريعةَ

لكى يتخذها مهنةً له. ٣- أعطنى كبايةً نظيفةً، وإلّا

أنهبُ وأشرب (نهبتُ وشربتُ) فى خان آخر. ٤-

لى مُوَيَّزَةٌ مستديرةٌ لأُمّى، وتشبهها إلّا أنَّ الألوانَ

قد ذبلت. ٥- كان الأقدَمون يبنون قصورهم ببروج

شامخة، ثم بعد مرور الزمان تغيّرت العادة؛ فَنَلْمَا

نرى بروجاً فى مبانى المعماريّة العصريين. ٦- اليوم

يُسَمِّى الأُمِّيُّونَ الدكتور "بالحكيم" لأنهم يعتـبرون

الحكمة من مِيفاته. ٧- أما علم الطب فَرُبَّما ابتـدأ

فى بلاد اليونان قبل المسيح بعدّة قرون (عدة قرون

قبل المسيح). ٨- قال قيصر: جئتُ، فرأيتُ، فغلبتُ.

وكان ذلك عندما رجع إلى ايطاليا من فرنسا بجيشه.

111

٩- كنت آكل فى بيته كثيرًا حتى انتقل إلى مدينة
أخرى ، ثم لم أَعُد أراه حتى يوم موته . ١٠- بينما ننظر
ارتفع للسماء فى سحاب .

Exercise 97

A

But in the Middle East there is a group of people who hate
the influence of the West. They say: "This influence has
given us nothing except lack of faith, and nothing has
resulted from it except denial of our traditions, customs and
history." This is what many inhabitants of those countries
believe. But they forget the tradition of the Prophet (May
God bless him and save him!): "Seek knowledge, even from
China."

B

All the members of the Government resigned except two of
them, (namely) the Foreign Minister, and the Minister of
Economy and Trade. These two, and other thoughtful
people among the inhabitants of the country, see great
danger in the rebels' demands. These, without doubt, will
harm the economy of the country, even though they arouse
the emotions of the masses.

C

Apart from the boys and girls, all the people of the village
have gone out to the fields (*lit.* sown, or cultivated, places);
for this is autumn, and this year's crops are very plentiful.
The reason is the heavy rains (*lit.* the plenty of the rains)
which fell in practically all months except the month of
March.

A

لكِنَّ هُنَاكَ فِي الشَّرْقِ الأَوْسَطِ فِئَةً يَكْرَهُونَ تَأْثِيرَ الغَرْبِ ،

فَيَقُولُونَ : مَا أَعْطَانَا هٰذَا التَّأْثِيرُ إِلَّا عَدَمَ الإِيمَانِ ، وَمَا

نَتَجَ عَنْهُ إِلَّا إِنْكَارُ تَقَالِيدِنَا وَعَادَاتِنَا وَتَأْرِيخِنَا. وَهٰـذَا مَا

يَعْتَقِدُهُ الكَثِيرُ مِنْ سُكَّانِ تِلْكَ البِلَادِ. لٰكِنَّهُمْ يَنْسَوْنَ حَدِيثَ

النَّبِيِّ (صلعم) : اُطْلُبِ العِلْمَ وَلَوْ مِنَ الصِّينِ .

B

اِسْتَقَالَ جَمِيعُ أَعْضَاءِ الحُكُومَةِ مَا عَدَا اثْنَيْنِ مِنْهُمْ ، هُمَا وَزِيرُ

الخَارِجِيَّةِ وَوَزِيرُ الإِقْتِصَادِ وَالتِّجَارَةِ: وَهٰذَانِ وَغَيْرُهُمَا

مِنَ المُفَكِّرِينَ مِنْ بَيْنِ سُكَّانِ البِلَادِ ، يَرَوْنَ خَطَرًا كَبِيرًا فِي

مَطَالِبِ الثُّوَّارِ؛ فَهِيَ ، وَلَا شَكَّ ، تُضِرُّ بِاقْتِصَادِ الدَّوْلَةِ، إِلَّا

أَنَّهَا تُثِيرُ عَوَاطِفَ العَامَّةِ .

C

إِلَّا الأَوْلَادَ وَالبَنَاتِ ، خَرَجَ جَمِيعُ نَاسِ القَرْيَةِ لِلْمَزَارِعِ ،

فَهٰـذَا فَصْلُ الخَرِيفِ وَمَحْصُولَاتُ هٰذِهِ السَّنَةِ وَافِرَةٌ جِدًّا،

وَٱلسَّبَبُ كَثْرَةُ ٱلْأَمْطَارِ ٱلَّتِي سَقَطَتْ فِي جَمِيعِ ٱلشُّهُورِ تَقْرِيبًا إِلَّا شَهْرَ آذَارَ (مَارِس).

A

انْتَظَرَ كُلُّ الْمَرْضَى الطَّبِيبَ فِي عِيَادَتِهِ عِدَّةَ سَاعَاتٍ إِلَّا أَحَدًا وَكَانَ هٰذَا الرَّجُلُ يَعْرِفُ عَادَاتِ الطَّبِيبِ . وَسَبَبُ تَأَخُّرِ الطَّبِيبِ أَنَّهُ، بَيْنَمَا يَرْجِعُ مِنْ زِيَارَةِ مَرِيضٍ مِنْ مَرْضَاهُ فِي بَيْتِهِ، وَقَفَ فِي طَرِيقِهِ إِلَى الْبَيْتِ عِنْدَ خَمَّارَةٍ لِيَشْرَبَ شَيْئًا . وَكَثِيرًا مَا كَانَ يَعْمَلُ ذٰلِكَ، لَا سِيَّمَا فِي الشِّتَاءِ . فَلِهٰذَا السَّبَبِ قَدْ فَقَدَ مَرْضَى كَثِيرِينَ . وَكَانَ فَقْدُهُ أَكْثَرَ، آلَّا (لَوْلَا) أَنَّهُ مَاهِرٌ وَذُو خِبْرَةٍ .

B

لَمَّا دَخَلْتُ بَيْتَ صَدِيقِي مَا رَأَيْتُ إِلَّا شَبَحًا، وَمَاكُنْتُ إِلَّا شَاِبًّا . فَأَخَافَنِي ذٰلِكَ الْمَنْظَرُ، وَمَا عَدَا أَبِي لَمْ أَرَ رَجُلًا مُحْتَضِرًا أَبَدًا . وَمَا كَانَ مَعَ صَدِيقِي أَحَدٌ إِلَّا خَادِمُهُ الْغَافِلُ الْقَلِيلُ الْخِبْرَةِ . لِذٰلِكَ عَزَمْتُ عَلَى أَنْ أَبْقَى مَعَهُ بُرْهَةً .

114

C

قد كان حسن يرغب في أن يقرأ «كتاب البخلاء» للجاحظ
وقال ذلك لأبيه. ثم عندما حَلّ عيدُ مولده (ميلاده) كان
ينتظر أن يعطيه أبوه نسخةً من ذلك الكتاب. لكنـه
أعطاه كتابًا آخر بدلاً منه ، فكان غضبانَ جدًّا برهـةً
من الزمان . ولمّا قرأ الكتاب أعجبه كثيرًا .

D

لم يدخل مدينتنا أقطّ غرباء إلّا عشرةُ مسافرينَ قد
أضاعوا طريقهم . فقُتل كلهم إلّا اثنين. وسمحنا لهما
بالبقاء لأنّ أحدهما حدّاد والآخر نجّار .

115

SUPPLEMENT

Selections from the Qur'ān

Sūra 1
Sūra of the Opening

In the name of God, the Merciful and the Compassionate. Praise be to God, Lord of the Worlds,[1] the Merciful, the Compassionate. Master of the Day of Judgement. Thee do we serve and from Thee do we ask help. Lead us in the straight path, the path of those to whom Thou art gracious, not of those to whom anger is shewn, nor of those who go astray.

Sūra 112
The Sūra of Unity[2]

Say: He is God, (the) One; God the Eternal; He did not beget, nor was He begotten; and none was His equal.

Sūra 113
Sūra of the Dawn

Say: I take refuge in the Lord of the dawn from the evil of what He has created, and from the evil of the darkening moon when it is in eclipse, and from the evil of the sorceresses who blow (spit) on knots,[3] and from the evil of an envious man when he envies.

---

[1] This is a literal translation of the original. Some authorities render it "Lord of Creation" or "Lord of Mankind".

[2] The fourth form verb akhlaṣa is frequently encountered in modern Arabic, meaning "to be faithful, devoted, sincere"; hence the use of the Active Participle at the end of letters, to give a meaning similar to the English expression "yours sincerely" (see pp. 494/5 of the Grammar). The Classical meaning of this verb is "to clarify, to act sincerely in". It is probable that the verbal noun in the title of this sūra means "acting sincerely (in religion), purifying oneself from polytheism", hence, "sincere belief in the one-ness *or* unity of God". In this sūra, as elsewhere in the Qur'ān, the Christian doctrine of the son-ship of Christ is attacked.

[3] A reference to a form of old Arabian witchcraft in which women tied knots in a cord and blew or spit upon them with an imprecation.

Sūra 114
Sūra of the People

Say: I take refuge in the Lord of the people, the King of the people, the God of the people from the evil of the whisperer (Satan)[1] who conceals himself, who whispers in the hearts of the people; and from the jinn[2] and the people.

Fables

From *Majānī al-'Adab* (Gleanings of Literature), by Louis Cheikho (A.D. 1859–1927).

THE WEASELS AND THE FOWLS

(News) reached the weasels that the fowls had fallen sick, so they put on peacocks' skins, and came to visit them. They said to them: "Peace be upon you, O fowls! How are you, and what condition are you in?" (*lit.* how are your conditions?) They said: "We are well on the day we don't see your faces". The moral of the story is (*lit.* its moral): Many show love outwardly and conceal (inward) hatred.

TWO CATS AND AN APE

Two cats snatched a piece of cheese, and took it to the ape to divide it between them. So he divided it into two parts, one of them larger than the other, and put them on his weighing scales; and the larger weighed down. Then he took a piece of it off with his teeth, showing that he wanted to make it equal to the smaller. But since what he took from it was larger than what was necessary, the smaller (now) weighed down. Then he did to this piece what he had done to the other, then he did to the other what he had done to

---

[1] Or suggester or prompter (of evil deeds).
[2] Demons.

this, and so on until the cheese was almost finished. The two cats said to him: "We are content with this division, so give us the cheese". He said: "If you are content, justice is not content"; and he kept on gnawing the heavier piece until he had finished all. So the cats returned in grief and disappointment, saying: "There is no power except the power of God above it, and no wrongdoer who is not afflicted by a greater wrongdoer."

A Hunter and a Sparrow

A hunter was hunting sparrows one cold day, and he was killing them while his tears flowed. One sparrow said to another: "There is no danger from that man. Do you not see him weeping?" The other said to him: "Do not look at his tears, but look at what his hands are doing".

A Negro

A negro in the winter-time began to take the snow and rub his body with it. He was asked: "Why (do you do) that?" He said: "In the hope that (*lit.* Perhaps) I may become white". A wise man said to him: "So-and-so, do not tire yourself. For perhaps the snow will become black from your body, while that remains as it was" (*lit.* in its condition). The moral is (*lit.* its moral): Evil can corrupt good, while rarely does evil improve good.

A Lion, a Fox, and a Wolf

(And) it is a parable about one who is exhorted by another and follows his example.

A lion, a fox, and a wolf were companions, and went out hunting, and they took an ass, a hare, and a gazelle. The lion said to the wolf: "Divide (it) among us". He (*i.e. the wolf*) said: "The matter is clear; the ass to the lion, the hare to

119

the fox, and the gazelle to me". And the lion struck him and made his head fly (off). Then he came to the fox and said: "How ignorant of booty your companion is! Come and tell (me) your opinion". He said: "O Abū l-Ḥārith,* the thing is clear; the ass for your breakfast, the gazelle for your lunch, and eat the hare between meals". The lion said to him: "What an excellent judge you are! Who taught you this law?" And he said: "The head of the wolf flying from his body".

A Fox and a Hyena

It is related that the fox was looking into a well, while thirsty: and over it was a rope at the ends of which were two buckets. So he sat in the upper bucket and descended and drank. The hyena came and looked into the well, and saw the moon in the water divided into two parts, and the fox was sitting at the bottom of the well. She said to him: "What are you doing down here?" He said to her: "I have eaten half of this cheese, and the other half remains for you, so come down and eat it". She said: "How shall I come down?" He said: "Sit in the bucket". So she sat in it and went down, and the fox was raised in the other bucket. And when they met in the middle (*i.e. half way down*) of the well, she said to him: "What is this?" He said: "Merchants go up and down like this". So the Arabs made of these two (*lit.* "them" *dual*) the proverb of one going up while another goes down (*lit.* about the two going in opposite directions).

The Story of the Ass and the Ox and the Farmer

(from *The Thousand and One Nights – the Arabian Nights*)

He (the story-teller) said: A certain merchant had wealth and cattle. He also had a wife and children. And Almighty

---

* *Abū l-Ḥārith* was a familiar nick-name for the lion. Ḥārith means a "collector of property", and the lion, as the finest beast of prey, was considered the best collector of food.

God had given him knowledge of the speech of animals and birds. That merchant lived in the country, and he had in his house an ass and an ox. One day the ox came to the donkey's place, and found it swept and sprinkled, and in his stall sifted barley and sifted straw, while he was lying down resting. At certain times, his master would ride him, as he needed, and then he would return to his (former) state. One day the merchant heard the ox say to the ass: "Good luck to you in that! I am tired, and you are resting, and you eat sifted barley, and they wait upon you. Sometimes your master rides you and returns, while I am always ploughing and grinding". The ass said to him: "When you go out to the field, and they put the yoke on your neck, lie down and don't get up. If they strike you and you rise, lie down a second time. When they bring you back and put the beans (down) for you, don't eat them, as if you were weak. Then abstain from eating and drinking for a day, or two or three. Then you will have relief (*lit.* rest) from fatigue and effort." The merchant was listening to what they said. So when the driver came to the ox to feed him, he ate only a very little. The driver went to take the ox ploughing, and found him weak. So the merchant said to him: "Take the ass and make him plough in his place for the whole day". So the man returned and took the ass in place of the ox, and made him plough instead of him the whole day. When he returned at the end of the day, the ox thanked him for his kindness, since he had rested him from fatigue during that day. The ass made no reply, and repented greatly.

When the next day came, the sower came and took the ass and made him plough till the end of the day, and the ass did not return until his neck was galled, and he was very weak. The ox looked at him, and thanked him and glorified him. The ass said to him: "I lived in ease, and only my kindness has injured me". Then he said: "You should know (*lit.* "know" – *imperative*) that I am a (good) adviser to you. Now I have heard our master say 'If the ox does not rise from his place, give him to the slaughterer to slaughter him and make his skin into leather'. I am afraid for you, and I am really giving you good advice" (*lit.* I am advising you, and peace). When the ox heard the words of the ass, he thanked him and said: "Tomorrow I will go out with them in the morning". Then the ox ate all his food, until he licked the manger with his tongue. (During) all this, their master was listening to what they said. So when day dawned, the merchant and his wife went out to the cattle shed and sat down. The driver came and took the ox and went out. And when the ox saw his master, he waved his tail, and broke wind, and was lively. The merchant laughed till he fell on the back of his head. His wife said to him: "What are you laughing at?" He said: "At something I have seen and heard, but I cannot reveal it or I should die". She said to him: "You must tell me that, and what is the cause of your laughing, even if you should die". He told her: "I cannot reveal it for fear of death". She said to him: "You were only laughing at me". Then she went on insisting to him and persisting in talking until she overcame him, and he was perplexed. So he summoned his children and sent for the judge and witnesses, and wished to make a will, and then reveal the secret to her, and then die. For he loved her greatly, because she was his cousin,* and the mother of his children, and he was a hundred and twenty years old.

Then he sent for all her family and the people of his quarter and told them his story, and that when he told anyone the secret he would die. All those present said to her: "We adjure you by God, desist from this matter, so that your husband, the father of your children, does not die". She said to them: "I will not give it up until he tells me, even if he die": so they said no more to her. Then the merchant rose and left them, and went to the stable to wash, (intending) to

---

* here, a euphemism for "wife", as if she were the daughter of his uncle. This is a phrase often used, arising from the custom of marrying within the family or clan.

return, tell them, and then die. Now he had a cock under which were fifty hens, and also a dog. He heard the dog calling the cock by his name (*lit.* calling him and naming him), and saying to him: "You are joyful and our master is going to die". The cock said to the dog: "And how is that?" The dog repeated the story to him, and the cock said to him: "Good heavens! Really our master is stupid. I have fifty wives. I please this one and anger that. As for him, he has only one wife and does not know how to deal with her (*lit.* making good his affair with her). Why does he not take one of the branches of the mulberry tree to her, then go into her room and beat her until she dies, or repents and stops asking him about anything?" When the merchant heard the cock's words, while talking to the dog, he returned to his senses and decided to beat her and enter her room, after cutting off for her a branch of the mulberry tree and hiding it in her room. Then he said to her: "Come into the room, so that I can tell you with no-one looking, and then die". She entered with him, and he shut the door of the room behind them and fell upon her with blows until she fainted. She said to him: "I repent (*lit.* have repented)." Then she kissed his hands and feet and repented, and went out with him. The company and her family rejoiced, and they lived happily ever after (*lit.* they sat in the happiest circumstances until death).

From the Prolegomena (Introduction) of Ibn K̲h̲aldūn (1332–1406 A.D.)

Concerning the Ways, Means, and Methods of Making a Living

You must know (*Imperative in the Arabic*) that "making a living" means the desire for sustenance and the striving to obtain it. It (the word) is of the form *maf ʿal* from (the root)

ʿaish. It is as if ʿaish, which is life, is only obtained by these (things), so they were considered, with some exaggeration, the place (of the act of making a living). Then again, the obtaining and gaining of sustenance may be by taking it from others' hands and appropriating it according to the generally accepted norm – this being called imposts and taxation. On the other hand, it may be (obtained) from wild animals by hunting them and shooting them on land or sea; this is called hunting. Again, it may be (obtained) from domesticated animals through the extraction of their surplus products which are used by people as sources of profit, such as milk from animals, silk from worms, and honey from bees; or it may be from plants which are planted and trees which are grown and prepared for the extraction of their fruits. All this is termed agriculture. Again, profit may come from human labour – either from specific materials, in which case it is termed crafts, such as writing, carpentry, tailoring, weaving, horsemanship, and the like – or unspecified materials; that is, all other professions and activities. Profit may also come from merchandise and preparing it for barter, either by travelling around with it in countries (or towns), or by hoarding it (cornering it) and waiting on (observing) the fluctuations of the market in it. This is called trade.

These are the ways and means of obtaining a living, and this is the meaning of what was mentioned by investigators among men of culture and wisdom like al-Ḥarīrī and others. They said that the making of a living is by ruling (others), trade, agriculture, and craftsmanship. As for ruling (others), it is not a natural means of livelihood, so it requires no mention. Something has been said in the second chapter about the circumstances of governmental taxation. As for agriculture, craftsmanship, and trade, they are natural means of livelihood. Agriculture is prior to all others by its very nature since it is simple and innately natural. It requires no consideration (speculation) or learning; it is therefore, ascribed to Adam, the father of mankind. He is said to have taught and undertaken it, indicating that it is the oldest way of making a living and the closest to nature. Now the crafts are secondary, coming later, as they are composite and scientific; thinking and speculation are applied to them. Consequently, as a rule, they are found only in sedentary communities which come after, and are secondary to, nomadism. In this sense they were ascribed to Idrīs, the second father of mankind. He discovered them for those who came after him by the revelation of Almighty God. Again, while trade is a natural way of making profit, most of its means and methods are contrivances to obtain the balance between purchase and sale prices in order to gain profit from that margin. For this reason the law permits rapacity in it since it has an element of gambling. But it does not constitute taking away the property of others without recompense. For this reason it was included in that which is legally permitted.

From the Cosmography of al-Qazwīnī (1203–1283 A.D.)

Baṣra

Baṣra is the famous city built by the Muslims. Al-Sha'bī said: Baṣra was built a year and a half before Kūfa. It is a city near the sea, plentiful in palms and (other) trees, with saline soil and salty water, because the tide coming from the sea goes up-stream to a distance of over three days' journey above Baṣra. When the water of the Tigris and Euphrates reaches Baṣra it mixes with the sea water, and thus becomes salty. As for its palm-trees, they are very plentiful. Al-Asma'ī said: I heard (Hārūn) al-Rashīd say: We looked, and behold! all the gold and silver on the face of the earth did not equal the value of Baṣra's palms. There are three remarkable things (about Baṣra). One of them is that the Tigris and

125

Euphrates join near Baṣra and become a great river which flows from the north side to the south: this they call the ebb. Then it flows back from the south to the north, and this they call the flow. It does that twice every day and night. When it ebbs it becomes greatly reduced so that if it were measured, the water which goes would be as much as that which remains, or more. At the beginning of every month it reaches its limit of increase, and waters the high places and distant lands. Then it begins to reduce (in quantity), and each day and night it is less than it was previously, until the end of the first week of the month. Then it begins to increase, and then every night and day it is more plentiful than before until the middle of the month. Then it begins to reduce, until the end of the week, and then to increase until the end of the month. (It is) always like this, and this rule neither ceases nor changes. The second remarkable thing is that if you were to look for a fly on its ripe fruit on the palms, or in its date-drying places, or date-presses, you would find (flies) in great numbers. And if a press is within the flood area or wine is made from a date tree under the dyke, you would not be able to see it clearly because of the abundance of flies. And people have mentioned this as being due to a spell. The third of them (*i.e.* the remarkable things) is that the crows migrating in autumn turn all the palms and (other) trees of Baṣra black so that not a branch can be seen without any on it. During the whole of that time one never finds a crow coming down on a palm-tree without (leaving it) stripped, even if (only) a single bunch of dates remained on it (previously). Crows' beaks are like picks, and the bunches of dates at that time are not firmly attached. So were it not for Almighty God's goodness, all of them would fall off from the crows' pecking. Then you await the time for gathering the dates (*lit.* them), and when the gathering is finished you see them also in between the roots of the stumps. Then, do not leave a (single) bad date without removing it. And praise be to Him (*i.e.* God) who ordained that out of kindness to his creatures.

From "Guidance of the Clever to Knowledge of the Learned"
(*Dictionary of Learned Men*) by Yāqūt (1179–1229 A.D.)

Isḥāq b. Ibrāhīm al-Mauṣilī

His kunya* was Abū Muḥammad, while (Hārūn) al-Rashīd,
when he wanted to show affection for him, called him Abū
Sufyān. If we wanted to do full justice to (*lit.* exhaust) his
status in knowledge and his place in literature and poetry, the
book would become (very) long; thus we would deviate from
our aim of brevity. And whoever is acquainted with the
stories and follows the traditions will ascertain his position.
Now singing was the least of his sciences, and the least
estimable ascribed to him: nevertheless it was the predomi-
nant one with him, for in the rest of his sciences he had
equals, whereas in this he had no equal – no-one coming
before him who outstripped him in it, and no-one coming
after who surpassed him.

He was the expert of this craft, although he of all people
most disliked singing and having anything to do with it. He
said: Whenever anyone inviting me wanted me to sing, or
someone said "Isḥāq al-Mauṣilī the *singer*", I wished I could
be beaten ten times (I could not bear more than that) and
could be excused from singing and from being associated
with it. Al-Ma'mūn used to say: Were it not for what men
had previously said about Isḥāq and his fame with them in
singing I would have appointed him judge in person (*lit.*
in my presence). For he is more suitable for this than these
judges, more deserving, more virtuous, more faithful in
religious observance and faith. He said: I remained for some
time visiting Hushaim, hearing the ḥadīth from him. Then
I went to al-Kisā'ī, reading with him part of the Koran; then
to al-Farrā', reading another part; then to Manṣūr Zalzal,
who would contend with me in two or three methods; then
to 'Ātika bint Shahda, from whom I would learn (*lit.* take)

---

* See page 359 in the Grammar.

a song or two. After that I would come to al-Aṣmaʿī and recite to him, and to Abū ʿUbaida and confer with him, then to my father and inform him what I had done, whom I had met, and what I had learned. I would have lunch with him, then when evening came, I would go to (see) al-Rashīd. Al-Aṣmaʿī said: I went out with al-Rashīd, and met Isḥāq al-Mauṣilī there.* I said to him: Have you brought (*lit.* carried) some of your book? He said: I have brought a little of it (*lit.* what is light). I said: What quantity is it? He said: Eighteen chests (full). I was astounded and said: If that is a little, how much is a lot? (*lit.* what is heavy). He said: Several times that.

From *The Book of Misers* by al-Jāḥiẓ (d. *c.*872 A.D.)

A Lie for a Lie

Similar to this story is what was told me by Muḥammad ibn Yasīr, about a governor who was in Persia – it may have been Khālid ibn Mahrawaih or someone else. He said: One day, while he was in his council chamber busy with his accounts and (other) affairs, and had concealed himself as much as he could, there appeared suddenly before him a poet who recited to him a poem praising him, eulogising him, and glorifying him (*i.e.* praising him to excess). When he had finished, he (the Governor) said: Well done! Then he approached his clerk, and said: Give him 10,000 dirhems. The poet was so happy that he almost flew into the air. When he (the Governor) saw his condition, he said: I see what I have said has moved you like this! Make it 20,000 dirhems. The poet almost jumped out of his skin. When he (the Governor) saw that his joy had doubled, he said: Your joy doubles when what I say (*lit.* the speech) doubles. Give him 40,000,

---

* "bihā" in the original is inexplicable, as there is nothing to which the pronominal suffix can be referred back.

So-and-so! (His) joy almost killed him (the poet). But when he came to his senses, he said to him (the Governor): You – may I be your ransom! – are a generous man. I know that as I increased in joy you increased the prize for me. But to accept this from you could only be out of lack of gratitude for it. Then he said: God bless you! (*lit.* he prayed for him) and went out.

He said: Then his clerk approached him and said: Good heavens! This (man) would have been content with 40 dirhems, and you order 40,000 dirhems for him! He (the Governor) said: Don't be stupid! (*lit.* Woe to you!) Do you want to give him anything? (The clerk) said: And is there any way out of carrying out your order? He said: You idiot! This man pleased us with (mere) words and we pleased him with words! When he claimed that I was more beautiful than the moon and stronger than the lion, and that my tongue was sharper than a sword, and that my command was more penetrating than lances, did he put into my hand thus anything (substantial) which I can recompense by something (substantial)? Don't we know that he lied? But he pleased us when he lied for us. So we please(d) him with speech and ordered rewards for him, despite his lying. Thus it will be lie for lie, and words for words. As for recompensing (*lit.* that it should be) lies by truth, and speech by deeds, this is the (sort of) loss I have never heard about.

From *Masterpiece of the Perspicacious concerning the Marvels of Cities and the Wonders of Travel*, by Ibn Baṭṭūta (A.D. 1304–1377).

I

When noon came, we heard talking at the water-tank, and they thought they were their companions (speaking). So they signalled me to go down with them. We went down and found there were other people. They made signs to them to accompany them, but they refused. Three of them sat in front of me, with me facing them. They put on the ground some hempen rope (which they had) with them. I watched them, saying to myself: "This is the rope with which they will tie me up when they kill me (*lit.* at the killing)". And I remained like that for an hour. Then (the) three of their companions who had captured me came, and they spoke with them, and I understood that they said to them: "Why have you not killed him?" The old man pointed to the negro, as if he were using his sickness as an excuse. Now one of these three was a handsome-faced youth, and he said to me: "Would you like me to set you free?" I said: "Yes!" He said: "Go!" So I took the jubba* I was wearing, and gave it to him; and he gave me a tattered blue cloak of his. Then he showed me the way, and I went off. I was afraid that they would see fit to pursue me, so I entered a sugar cane thicket and hid in it till the sun set. Then I came out and followed the road which the youth had shown me. It led me to water, and I drank some of it. I went on until a third of the way through the night, and reached a mountain, and went to sleep at the foot of it. When I woke up next morning, I followed the road (further), and, in the forenoon, reached a high rocky mountain, on which were sweet lote and lotus trees. I went on picking the† fruit and eating it, so much so that the thorns made marks on my arms which remain to this day.

II

Then that road led to the villages of the unbelievers. So I followed another road, which took me to a ruined village. In it I saw two naked negroes, and was frightened of them, so I settled down beneath some trees there. When night fell

---

* A long cloak.
† See vocabulary in "A New Arabic Grammar".

I entered the village and found somewhere to stay (*lit.* an abode, house) in one of their houses shaped like large jars, which they erect (*lit.* put) for storing produce, at the base of which was a hole which would take a man (*lit. the* man). I entered it, and found its interior strewn with straw, and among the straw were stones on which I placed my head and went to sleep. High in it (*lit.* above it) was a bird which flapped its wings most of the night; I think it was afraid, so we were both equally afraid. I remained in that condition seven days from the day on which I was captured, which was a Saturday.

From *The Conquest of Andalusia* (*Spain*), by Jirji Zaidän (A.D. 1861–1914)

Andalusia, the Goths, and Toledo

Andalusia is one of the provinces of Spain, its name being originally "Vandalusia", in derivation from the Vandals who had settled there after the Romans. When the Arabs conquered it they called it Andalusia (al-Andalus); they then applied this name to the whole of Spain.

Spain was part of the Western Roman Empire until the fifth century A.D. Then it was assaulted by the Goths who belonged to the Germanic tribes who had travelled from the heights of India to Europe in search of pastures and a livelihood. They settled in the steppes of Europe,* as the Arabs settled in the deserts* of Syria and Iraq. Then the Goths assaulted the Western Roman Empire a few centuries before the Arabs attacked the Eastern (Roman) Empire, and founded kingdoms in France, Germany, and England,

---

*The Arabic word for "desert" can be applied to any extensive waste land. Hence here it means "steppes" in the first instance, and "desert" in the second.

and other (countries). These are states which still exist in Europe.

Among those tribes was the tribe of the Western Goths ("Visigoths") who attacked Spain in the fifth century and took it from the Romans. They founded in it a Gothic kingdom which came to an end with the Islamic conquest in 92 A.H. (A.D. 711) at the hands of Ṭāriq ibn Ziyād, the famous Berber commander.

At that time (year) the capital of the Gothic kingdom in Spain was the city of Toledo, on the banks of the River Tagus, in central Spain. At that period Toledo was a flourishing city in which were fortresses, citadels, palaces, churches, and monasteries. It was the centre of religion and politics. Every year there took place an assembly of all the bishops to look into matters of general interest (*lit.* general matters).

The king of Spain in the year of the conquest was Roderic, whom the Arabs call Lotheric (Ludhrīq). He was of Gothic descent, and he succeeded to the throne. He was not of the ruling dynasty, but had usurped the throne, leaving the sons of the former king to take vengeance on him. At that time Spain was divided into provinces or duchies. Each of its duchies was ruled by a governor called the "duke" or the "count". In their rule they were all subordinate (*lit.* they returned to) the king who resided in Toledo.

Toledo was situated on high ground consisting of hillocks encompassed by the River Tagus on all sides except the north, thus resembling (in shape) a horseshoe exactly. Beyond the river on the East, West, and South were ranges of mountains which hid the horizon from the people of the city. In them were olive groves and vineyards and forests of oak and pine. In the centre of the town was the cathedral (*lit.* the biggest church) which the Muslims turned into a mosque after the conquest. It was of considerable beauty and strength. If one looked down on the buildings of Toledo from a height one would see in the kinds of buildings a mixture of Roman and Gothic styles. Around the city to the

132

north, and beyond the city in other directions, were planta-
tions of fruit-trees* and other types of trees. If one stood
and looked out of one of the windows of the houses one
would (be able) to look down on them all.

From *Al-Ayyām* (The Days), an autobiography by Ṭaha
Ḥusain (A.D. 1891–   ).

I saw you, my daughter, one day, sitting on your father's lap,
while he told you the story of Oedipus Rex, when he (the
latter) left his palace, after putting out his eyes, and did not
know how to walk (*lit*. go). And his daughter Antigone came
and led and guided him. I saw you on that day listening to
this story happily at the start of it. Then your colour began
to change little by little, and your smooth brow began to
pale gradually. Soon you burst into tears and fell prostrate
on your father, embracing and kissing (him).† Your mother
came and took you from his arms and kept you until your
fear was calmed. Your mother understood, and your father
also, and I too understood, that you cried because you saw
Oedipus Rex like your father, blind, sightless, unable to
move unaided. So you wept for your father as you wept for
Oedipus.

The women in the villages of Egypt do not like silence, nor
do they incline towards it. If one of them is left alone and
finds no-one to talk to, she speaks to herself in various ways.
If she is happy she sings; if she is sad she eulogises the dead.
And every woman in Egypt can be sad whenever she wants.
When the women of the villages are left alone, the thing they

---

* In the Arabic here two synonyms are used for "fruits".
† The Arabic here has two different words for kissing, but as there is
no suitable synonym in English, the first word is here translated as
"embracing".

133

like best is to mention their pains and their dead, and to eulogise (the latter). This eulogising of the dead frequently ends in real weeping. Our friend (*i.e.* the author, Ṭaha Ḥusain) was the happiest of people when listening to his sisters while they sang, and to his mother while she eulogised the dead.

His sisters' singing used to anger him, and leave no impression on his soul (*or* on him), for he found it silly and meaningless; while his mother's keening stirred him strongly and frequently made him cry. In this way did our friend learn many of the songs and elegies, and many stories, both serious and amusing.

From *The Diary of a Legal Officer in Rural Areas*, by Taufīq al-Ḥakīm (A.D. 1898–   ).

I saw the driver hiding behind the trunk of the acacia tree, his face drawn, and his eyes popping out (*lit.* prominent of eyes), gazing on this scene, unable to control his feelings.
*"There is no power nor might except with God! To God we belong and to him do we return!" (he exclaimed).

The doctor caught sight of him and ordered him to keep away. I, too, shouted at the driver, after which he went off back to the car and crouched in it. What had frightened him? Was it the sight of the bones themselves? Or the idea of death which they represented? Or human destiny which he had seen before him with his own eyes? Why did the sight of corpses no longer affect people like myself and the doctor; and even people like the grave diggers and the sextons (*lit.* guards) in this way? It seemed to me that these corpses and bones had lost their symbols for us. To us they are no more than pieces of wood, or sticks of firewood, clay moulds or baked bricks.

---

* An expression of wonder.

They are things we handle (*or* deal with) in our daily work. They have lost that "symbolism" which is the basis of all our power. Yes; and what remains of these things, great and hallowed, which are all important in our human existence if we take away from them that "symbolism"? Does their remain nothing of them before our careless unheeding eyes but a body of matter – stones or bones of no significance or meaning? What is the destiny of mankind, and what is its value if it loses this "symbolism"? It is, in its essence, a being which has no (real) existence. It is nothing, yet it is everything in our earthly life. This "nothing" on which we base all our human life, is all the superiority we possess on value if it loses this "symbolism"? It is, in its essence, a being which has no (real) existence. It is nothing, yet it is everything in our earthly life. This "nothing" on which we base all our human life, is all the superiority we possess on which we can pride ourselves, and which distinguishes us from other creatures. This is the whole difference between the higher and the lower animals.

The doctor broke the course of my thoughts with his forceps, held in a hand wearing transparent skin gloves, with which he probed the bones.

From the novel *Sarah*, by 'Abbās Maḥmūd al-'Aqqād (A.D. 1889–   ).

The Meeting

Hammām found himself, as he was returning home, near the residence of his friend Professor Zāhir, who was a charming, good-natured man. At that time he lived in a house of furnished rooms, supervised by a French dressmaker called Marianne. Hammām sauntered along to the house to visit his friend and spend some time with him in conversation jumping from one topic to another, and laughing a lot in a way which, if it contained no wit of a high order, undoubtedly afforded the lungs beneficial exercise.

He found Marianne in the courtyard of the house, feeding her turkey with a plate of stale macaroni. With her was a pretty girl whose age was difficult to estimate, because she might be twenty, just as she might be twenty-five, and she might well be called "Miss" as she might be called "Mrs. (Madam)". She was busy with a dress which she was turning over and examining carefully.

Hammām said: "Good morning! Where is Zāhir, madam?" She returned the greeting, and said: "Do we only see you when you visit Zāhir? He went out a little while ago, but will return shortly".

Hammām looked at the plate of macaroni, saying: "I see that the fowl is today not Turkish* but Italian". Marianne replied only with a broad smile. But the girl replied saying: "If nationality were according to food, the fowl here are international, not belonging to any particular race. They are Egyptian when they eat casserole beans, English when they eat potatoes, and Indian when they put up with long fasting".

Marianne gave her a look of pretended reproach. But Hammām found her reply charming, and at the same time wondered at her participation in the conversation. Yet he welcomed this participation which he felt immediately to his liking, and he led the conversation to her, though tentatively (*lit.* slowly).

Hammām said: "Mademoiselle knows all about domesticated fowl, and their fickle nationality; but, mademoiselle, I don't remember seeing you here before".

What was he saying? Was he saying: "I don't remember seeing you"? Was it conceivable, then, that he might see her, and take no notice of her, and thus forget having seen her?

---

* *lit.* Roman, because what now constitutes most of Turkey, that is, Asia Minor, was part of the Eastern Roman (Byzantine) Empire, and was called al-Rūm by the Arabs. The turkey is still called "dīk rūmī", though sometimes also "dindin", by the Arabs.

Hammām, also, realised that his words did not coincide
with her wish, and he heard her reply with suppressed anger,
as if talking to herself: "Why do you address me as mademoiselle? Do you think me young? I am a housewife and a
mother!"

From the *Abridged History of Tunisia*, by Ḥasan Ḥusni 'Abd-
al-Wahhāb al-Ṣumādiḥi' (A.D. 1883–   ).

In 897 A.H. the Christians, under the hand of Ferdinand the
Catholic Lord of Castile, wrested Granada from its rulers
(kings) the Bani al-Aḥmar. At that time a great number of
Andalusian Muslims emigrated to the West and the East.
Many of the weak among them remained in their homes,
despised for their beliefs and persecuted in their rights, until
the beginning of the eleventh century A.H. Then the
Spaniards fell upon them with savagery and expelled them
all from their homes after punishing them cruelly, and drove
them into final exile. After innumerable hardships some of
them settled in the Maghrib (Morocco) because of its
proximity to their homeland. Others made for the land of
Tunis (Tunisia) because of the news they had received of
its people's generosity and the fertility of its soil. And so
they came, fleeing with their religion and faith to this land
from the year 1016 onwards. Their first arrival was in the
reign of 'Uthmān Dey. He welcomed the coming of these
afflicted people and softened their exile, and urged the people
of the capital to treat them kindly and so made them forget
the loss of their homeland.

Then this Dey assigned the imigrants from Andalusia the
lands they chose, and distributed among their needy property
and money. So they spread among the (various) parts of the
country, building villages and establishing farms and
orchards, till they restored the country's lost prosperity and
its past wealth. Among (the towns) they founded were:

137

Sulaimān, Qurunbāliya, al-Judaida, Zaghwān, Ṭiburba, Majāz al-bāb, Tastūr, Qal'at al-Andalus, and so on. In addition to that, a good number of them settled in the capital city of Tunisia, and there took over quarters which became associated with them, and markets for the crafts which they brought with them, such as the making of red felt caps, silk spinning, and the carving of marble, lime-stone and coloured tiles. The local people learned the elements of these trades from them and became expert in them. Altogether, the region acquired ample prosperity and great wealth from the emigration of the Andalusians.

From *The Sieve*, by Mīkhā'īl Nu'aima (A.D. 1894–)

The Drama and the Question of Language

The biggest obstacle I encountered in writing "Fathers and Sons" was the colloquial language and the place it should be given in plays such as these. To my way of thinking – and I think many will agree with me on this – the characters of a play must speak in the language in which they are accustomed to expressing their emotions and thoughts. The writer who tries to make an illiterate peasant speak in the language of poetical collections and philological works offends his peasant, himself, his reader, and his hearer. Indeed, he makes his characters appear comical where he does not intend to be comical, and commits a crime against an art, the beauty of which (lies) in depicting man as we see him in the real situations of life.

There is another matter deserving of attention concerning colloquial language – it is that this language, beneath its harsh exterior (*lit*. clothes) embodies much of the people's philosophy, their experience of life, their proverbs, and their convictions; and if you tried to put them in Classical language you would be like someone translating poetry and proverbs from a foreign language. We may be opposed in

138

this by those who carry dictionaries around (*lit.* under their arms), and arm themselves with books about accidence and grammar, all of whom say that "there are all kinds of game in the belly of the wild ass", and that in the colloquial language there is no eloquence, excellence or elegance which you cannot express in the classical language. These (individuals) we recommend to study assiduously and minutely the life and language of the people.

Drama, of all literary genres, cannot do without the colloquial language. Indeed, the dilemma is that, were we to follow this principle, we would have to write all our plays in the colloquial language, since there is no-one among us who speaks the Arabic of the Jāhilīya (pre-Islamic Arabia) or the early Islamic age, and that would mean the extinction of our Classical language. Yet we by no means desire this national catastrophe. So what is the way out (solution)?

I have sought the solution of this problem in vain, for it is too great for a single mind to solve. The gist of the conclusion I have come to, after (some) thought, is to make the educated among the characters of my play speak correct Arabic (*lit.* Arabicised language) and the illiterate speak the colloquial language. But I fully realise that this system does not solve the basic problem. Thus the matter still needs the attention of the greatest philologers and writers.

From *A Tear and a Smile*, by Jibrān Khalīl Jibrān (A.D. 1883–1931).

The Voice of the Poet

I yearn for my country because of its beauty, and I love the people of my country because of their misfortune. But if my people were driven by what they call patriotism, and marched against a neighbouring land, and despoiled its wealth, killed its men, orphaned its children, widowed its women, watered its soil with the blood of its children, and fed its wild animals with the flesh of its youth, then I would hate my country and the inhabitants of my country.

I am rejuvenated by the remembrance of my birthplace, and I long for the house in which I was raised. But if a wayfarer called (*lit.* passed) and asked for shelter in that house, and food from those living in it, and was refused and turned away, I would change my lauding to lamenting and my longing to indifference, and would say to myself: "The house which withholds bread from him who needs it, and a bed from him who seeks it, is, of all houses, most deserving of destruction and ruin".

I love the place in which I was born with some of my love for my country. I love my country with a part of my love for my native land. I love the earth as a whole because it is the pasture ground of humanity, the spirit of divinity on earth; that humanity which stands among ruins, whose naked form is clothed in tattered rags, on whose pallid cheeks flow abundant tears, which calls its children in a voice that fills the air with lamenting and wailing, while its children are made oblivious of its call by songs of (sectarian) bigotry, and distracted from its tears by the polishing of swords; that humanity which sits alone, asking succour of people, and they hear not. If anyone does hear it, approach it, wipe away its tears, and comfort it in its afflictions, people say: "Leave him, for tears affect only the weak".

Humanity is the spirit of divinity upon earth – that divinity which goes among the nations speaking of love, pointing out ways of life, while people laugh and scoff at its words and teachings; that which the Nazarene (Jesus) heard yesterday, so they crucified him; and Socrates, so they poisoned him; that (spirit) which has been heard today by those who speak in (the name of) Jesus and Socrates, and have made mention of it before the people, and the people cannot kill them – but they mock at them, saying: "Mockery is more cruel and bitter than killing".

140

Jerusalem was not strong enough to kill Jesus, and he lives for ever. Athens was not (strong enough) to destroy Socrates, and he lives for ever. Nor can mockery prevail against those who listen to humanity and follow the lead of divinity. They, too, shall live for ever and ever.

Specimen of modern Arabic verse from *Al-Jadāwil* (The Brooks) of Eliya Abū Mādī (A.D. 1889–1957).

I Do Not Know

I have come, I know not whence, but I have come,
And I have seen a road ahead of me, and have taken it.*
I will remain travelling, whether I wish this or not.
How have I come? How did I see my road? . . . .
      I do not know.

Am I new or old in this life?
Am I free and unfettered, or do I go in bonds?
Am I my own leader in my life, or am I led?
I would that I knew, but . . .
      I do not know.

Proverbs and Aphorisms

Proverbs are the lamps of speech (*lit.* speeches).
Haste is from the Devil, and delay from the Compassionate
    (*i.e.* God).
There is benefit in repetition (or, in reconsideration).
The good man may become evil.
The (confirmed) liar may (sometimes) tell the truth.
The drunkard's essay is read in the inn.
Four wives, and the water-skin is dry!

---

* *lit.* I walked.

Youth is the riding beast of ignorance (folly).

Speaking the truth has left me friendless.

Every young girl admires her father.

Speak to people according to their intelligence.

Every stranger is related to (every other) stranger.

A promise is (like) a cloud, a deed is (like) rain.

The excuse is worse than the offence.

Culture adorns the rich and hides the poverty of the poor.

Ugliness is a woman's protection (*lit.* protector, guardian).

Men are moulded by circumstances.

Everything is habit, even worship.

Evil is old.

$\left.\begin{array}{l}\text{He}\\\text{It}\end{array}\right\}$ left us, and we rejoiced, but $\left.\begin{array}{l}\text{someone}\\\text{something}\end{array}\right\}$ more unpleasant than $\left.\begin{array}{l}\text{it}\\\text{him}\end{array}\right\}$ came to us.

Do not trust the prince if the minister has cheated you.

Live, (and you will) see.

How many a saint's burial place is visited (by pilgrims), while its occupant is in (Hell-) fire.

Idleness and laziness taste sweeter than honey.

Look after your tongue: if you protect it, it will protect you: if you betray it, it will betray you.

Were it not for him who brought me up, I should not know my Lord (*i.e.* God).

SELECTIONS FROM THE ARABIC PRESS

From *al-Ahrām*, daily newspaper, Cairo

Fauzi flies to Accra to carry out the African Pact
Seven Experts fly out to set up the Permanent
Machinery for the Summit Conference

It has been decided that Dr. Mahmud Fauzi, Foreign Minister, will fly to Accra to attend the meeting of Foreign

Ministers which will be held in the middle of next month when the permanent machinery of the African Pact will be set up. The Pact was signed by President Gamal Abdel-Nasser (Jamāl 'Abd al-Nāṣir) in Casablanca last January with the leaders of the African States.

Experts from the seven African States which took part in the Casablanca Conference will fly to Accra early next month to hold a preparatory meeting of Foreign Ministers to agree on the details of the setting up (composition) of political, military, economic, and cultural committees, and the permanent Secretariat of the Pact.

The (United) Arab Republic will be represented at this meeting by seven Arab experts in the political, military, economic, and cultural fields, under the leadership of Mr. Maḥmūd Riyāḍ, adviser to the President of the Republic. This preparatory meeting will be held in the first week of next month. At its conclusion it will be turned into a conference at Foreign Ministers' level.

New Organisation (Reorganisation) for the Ministry of Local Administration
Five General Directors will head the Technical Administrations

A scheme has been completed for the organisation of the Ministry of Local Administration. The Ministry will consist of five administrations: the administrations of financial, departmental, and legal matters, of public relations, and technical inspection. These administrations will be headed by a director-general or a first-grade official. The Ministry will include technical sections concerned with the investigation of matters referred to the Ministry by the National Assembly or the National Union, or the various ministries.

The Ministry will not include administrations representing the technical supervisory (control) bodies in the provinces. For the supervision of the various executive ministries over the technical aspects of the local councils will remain in such a way that the governor will be under the control of a deputy for each minister who will supervise technically those aspects connected with the work of the Ministry. The administrations and technical departments will be supplied with their requirements of officials by means of the officials of the joint units, and the municipal and governmental administrations which have been incorporated in the Ministry of Local Administration from other ministries.

From *Akhbār al-yaum*, Cairo

The Policy of Planning

This (i.e. what has been said before) is from one point of view. From another, the State has adhered to a policy of economic and social planning, and, under this policy the general budget is no longer anything but one stage of the plan which the Government has laid down with all its ramifications. The government has also discussed it at various levels, and issued a general directive on the basis of it. Thus it has become restricted in every single little detail (*free translation*) so that any adjustment in the budget becomes a deviation from it contrary to the principle of the plan and in opposition to it. Indeed, (such an adjustment) might complicate the course of the plan, which is based on priority of the most important over the important, and providing the necessary possibilities of carrying out plans at a series of specified times. All this must be in accordance with the requirements of the (fixed) order of schemes and works, and within the bounds of the policy of the State and the various sectors.

This new policy which al-Qaisūni is following in preparing the State budget will prevent irregularities which took place in the past when the Chamber of Deputies used to increase the provisions of the budget without asking the government.

But it – the new policy – will not prevent the National Assembly from discussing with the Government any adjustment (modification) it considers should be included. If it (the Government) agrees upon it – within the framework of the broad plan, of course – it can be carried out within the limits of the constitution.

The purpose of all this is to make discussion in the National Assembly positive and useful.

From *al-Ḥayāt*, daily newspaper, Beirut

The Administration Committee will meet on Saturday at noon to begin the study of the rents scheme

From the special correspondent (representative) of *al-Ḥayāt*. It was anticipated that the Committee of Administration and Justice would meet today, Thursday, to study the new bill on rents. But this meeting has been deferred to noon next Saturday.

The Chairman of the committee, Shai<u>kh</u> Bahīj Taqīy al-Dīn, justified this delay by saying that the desire to invite all the representatives of the committee of tenants, the trade unions and the bodies (organisations) interested (*or* concerned with), and the landlords had necessitated postponing the appointed time to Saturday, in order to facilitate the invitation to them to attend the session and learn their views.

And, in fact, the office of the Council yesterday took in hand the sending of invitations to these representatives, reminding them of the necessity of preparing their memoranda about the demands which they are making (*lit.* calling for).

In yesterday's edition (*lit.* number) we referred to (the fact) that the workers' unions met and decided unanimously to reject the scheme on principle (*lit.* from its foundation).

Clash in Baalbek and the apprehension of those responsible (*lit.* the doers)

Because of a quarrel over the guarantee of some land in Ḥalabtā (the district of Baalbek), Da"ās Ṭa"ān Dandash and his son Naufal, and Khalīl Sa'īd 'Alā' al-Dīn, all of them from Zabūd, made an assault on Nā'if Saif al-Dīn. The latter claimed that they drew upon him weapons which they were carrying. On the same day, out of revenge for their kinsman, the said Nā'if, Muḥammad Dīb Saif al-Dīn and 'Alī Mahdī Saif al-Dīn waylaid Da"ās and his son. The police of Baalbek have carried out an investigation and arrested Khalīl 'Alā' al-Dīn, Muḥammad Saif al-Dīn, and Mahdī Saif al-Dīn, and searched their homes, without coming across anything prohibited. Active steps are being taken to arrest Da"ās.

From *al-'Alam*, daily newspaper, Rabat (Morocco)

The Ambassador of Morocco thanks the Iraqi Government and People

His Excellency the Moroccan Ambassador in Baghdad issued the following statement yesterday: The Ambassador of the Kingdom of Morocco in Iraq tenders his profound thanks and feelings to the noble Iraqi people, and to His Excellency the President of the Iraqi Assembly, and the minister and members of the diplomatic missions accredited to Iraq; to their honours the 'Ulamā' and the religious leaders; to representatives of political organisations and parties and representatives of trades unions and social bodies, journalists and women's organisations, and everyone bereaved by the death of the late departed King Muḥammad V – both those who were good enough to visit the Embassy at the time of the recitation of the *Fātiḥa* (opening chapter of the Qur'ān) and those who expressed their sympathies in telegrams and letters. To all these he conveys his deepest thanks and emotions for their expressions of sympathy and feelings of sorrow for the lamented deceased (King) of Morocco. These were the greatest consolation to him and the members of the Moroccan Embassy for this great tragedy which descended on the Moroccan people. He prays to Almighty God to preserve them and save them from (*lit.* not to show them) misfortune and evil.

From *al-Barq*, Arabic weekly, Paris

Agricultural Reform in Algeria

Agricultural reform has entered its constructive stage, after the establishment of a fund to help in the acquisition of agricultural land. The transfer has been completed of more than a thousand hectares which belonged to government or company estates. Thus, 66,000 hectares have been taken from the Algerian Company, and 16,000 hectares from the Swiss Company in Geneva; so the total has reached 100,000 hectares which will be divided into holdings (*or* plots) with an area varying between 15 and 25 hectares.

In those regions which have the advantage of irrigation sequestration will be carried out of those lands exceeding 50 hectares in area, or, where there are children, (estates shall) not exceed 150 hectares. As for the 20,000 hectares obtained, they will be distributed in plots of five hectares. ·Those who obtain these plots will be associated with a co-operative and a reserve agricultural company. And they need not necessarily be Muslims.

ADVERTISEMENTS AND
ANNOUNCEMENTS

The 'Alawīya Factories under the proprietorship
of Muhammad Ḥusain al-'Alawī

Al-'Alawīya Factories are ready to offer any assistance regarding "al-'Alawīya" machines. Should you have any
problem (difficulty), ideas, or complaint concerning this
product which you have purchased, or any enquiry about
other matters regarding this product, please inform us.

Guarantee

We certify that the manufacture of the "al-'Alawīya"
machine is guaranteed against any fault or blemish. This
guarantee will be considered void if any fault should develop
in it arising out of ill-use (misuse) of the machine or lack of
care, or its being repaired by any person who is not an agent
for the "al-'Alawīya" machine. This certificate is to be considered the sole guarantee. It must be returned with the
machine in the event of request for any service covered
by the guarantee, otherwise no repair will be considered
free.

The improvements which have taken place in the production
of "Vidor" batteries will pave the way for the resumption of
trade with world markets. It is within the capacity of this
well-known company to produce dry batteries suitable for all
purposes. It is also producing many kinds of the most up-to-
date radio sets and a great number of household electrical
appliances. The "Vidor" Company will be pleased to furnish
its overseas clients with details of its products and terms of
trade.

148

The Muḥammad 'Ali Bookshop for the Printing and Sale of Oriental Books

We have a large number of books (new and second-hand) from Egypt, Arabia, Turkey, Iran, India, China, etc., in all languages. Catalogues will be sent on request.

To authors and publishers: Please inform us of your publications.

Specialists in Fine Prints, Manuscripts, Pottery, and other products of India and Iran.

A Company of World Repute

requires qualified (capable) engineers and chemists who wish to take up industry as a career. Those interested (*lit.* willing) must be prepared to work in Beirut or Jidda (Kingdom of Saudi Arabia). The successful (applicants) will receive the necessary training on full pay before taking up their duties.

Applications should be sent to Post Office Box 1001, Beirut, before 15th March.

The Kingdom of Morocco
Ministry of National Economy
Office of Control and Export
Notice regarding submission of tenders

The Office of Control and Export, 72 Muhammad Smīḥa Street, Casablanca, will accept tenders up to the 18th March 1961 for the supply of clothing suitable for office messengers.

Official forms and further instructions can be obtained from the stores department of the office at the above-mentioned address.

Tenders must be sent to the Office Administration M.M.T. (*initials of the Arabic for "Moroccan Export Office"*) in a double envelope sealed with gum and registered. The outer envelope must have written on it the trade name of the tenderer with the words "Advertisement for Tenders regarding Clothing".

Notice

Required by the Ministry of the Interior – Department of Vehicle and Machine Registration – two Jeeps, year_ of manufacture 1960 or 1961.

Ten o'clock, Saturday, March 25th, 1961, has been fixed as the final date for offers by tender.

Tenders should be sent to the office of the administration of tenders, Manṣūr Salāma Building, Chateaubriand Street, before 12 o'clock on Friday, March 24th, 1961.

The register of conditions (terms) can be seen in the Comptroller's office of the (Ministry of) the Interior.

Notice

Newly offered for sale by public auction the whole government plot (estate) No. 539, of the area Burj al-Shamālī, Tyre, consisting of treeless land watered by streams (*or* other natural sources) for grain growing with an area of 3285 square metres.

The auction will take place in Tyre at the Sole Arbitrator's office from nine to eleven o'clock, Thursday 30th March 1961.

The list of conditions (terms) may be seen at the Directorate of Land Affairs in Beirut, the Department of State Property, Parliament Building. Also in the Secretariat of Land Registration in Sidon, and in the office of the Assistant Registrar of Lands in Tyre during official hours.

Intending buyers should attend at the appointed time together with the security (deposit) laid down in the list of conditions.

Tenders and Bids

(Office of) the Supervision of Town and Village Affairs in
Buḥaira Province. Tenders will be accepted up to Monday,
27/3/61 for the work of building the agricultural unit in the
District of Rosetta. Documents should be applied for from
the Supervision (Office) in Damanhūr on paper carrying
stamp value fifty milliemes, on payment of the sum of
8.500 Egyptian Pounds. The sum of 300 milliemes should be
added to it if documents are requested by post. Any tender
which is not accompanied by a deposit of two per cent of its
value, or is contrary to (not in accordance with) the terms of
the specifications and general conditions will not be considered.

Correspondence

NOTE: Much Arabic correspondence is in a florid style, and it is im-
possible to give a literal translation into the English of many of the
courtesy titles, forms of address, and greetings without distortion of
language.

My dear Mr. So-and-So,

After asking after your condition (health), we hope that
you are in the best of health at all times. We convey to you
our best wishes on the occasion of the coming New Year. We
would very much like to see you and visit the beautiful
capital of your country during these days of Christmas. I shall
write you a long letter during the course of the week. Give
our greetings to all our friends. And from me a thousand
greetings to you.

Yours sincerely,
So-and-So

Dear Mr. So-and-So,

After greeting you and hoping that you are in the best of
health, we were honoured to receive your letter dated the
14th and thank you very much. We have taken note of its

contents (*lit.* what you have explained in it has become known to us). As for the goods which you have at present, as we have already informed you we are interested in all kinds. We are able to offer them in the markets of Syria and import them; in particular those things which are of recent invention. We request you, should it be possible for you, to dispatch by post the small order as shown below. We would also request you to inform us of the price so that we can transmit the cost through one of the banks in your area.

My brother will write you today; he is in perfect health. All of us here speak very well of you and send you kindest greetings. In conclusion, please accept our sincerest greetings and thanks.

Yours etc.
So-and-So

To our very dear cousin,

Greetings! We hope that you are perfectly fit and well. Your kind letter dated the sixth of last month reached us most opportunely and we thank you very much. As for the English papers which you promised to send, they have not yet arrived, and I do not know the reason for the delay. I went to the post-office today and an official there told me that the plane from England was late because of fog over Rome airport, and that they had no news of its arrival (when it would arrive). Yesterday we were visited by our mutual friend, Mahmud Salim, on his way to New York, where he will take his brother's place in the consulate there. He stayed with us about two hours. His presence gave us great pleasure since we had not seen him for a long time, and we are very fond of him. We all accompanied him to the airport outside the city.

We hope that you will all continue in the best of health, and accept from us sincerest greetings; and long life to you!

Yours sincerely,
So-and-So